ANYONE CAN COACH

ANYONE CAN COACH

Transform Your Life
by Coaching Others to Excellence

Sean Mize

Printed in the United States of America

liferesultspublishing.com

ISBN: 978-0-9848586-0-6

First Printing Trade Paperback Edition 2012

To my Mom who introduced me to Jesus, encouraged me to think deeply before I was old enough to know I could, passed down an inheritance of strong internal motivation, and instilled in me a confidence that I can do anything I set my mind to. Thank you, Mom!

Contents

“Somewhere in your makeup lies sleeping, the seed of achievement which, if aroused and put into action, would carry you to heights, such as you may never have hoped to attain.”

- Napoleon Hill

Preface

One of the greatest joys in life is to be able to discover and fulfill one's purpose; another is to guide and empower others, through sharing one's own insight learned from experience and training, to achieve their goals and fulfill their purposes. Another great joy is to implement a dream that is so strong and has so much meaning that one is inspired to take massive action to bring into existence the manifestation of that dream. And yet, the pursuit of those joys and dreams is often impeded by a lack of knowledge of the steps to achieving them, the absence of a suitable role model or pattern to follow, or life circumstances that detract from the pursuit of personal goals and dreams; and for many people, those joys and dreams are non-existent as a result.

Many people the world over are stuck in a pattern of not being able to achieve all they would like to. Some are stuck in a corporate job that leaves them very little time for family, recreation, or a meaningful and fulfilling lifestyle. Others are stuck in a meaningless job, or are perhaps jobless, and try as they might, they can't envision a way to start a home or online business that will give them the financial freedom to pursue higher levels of freedom—such as recreation, a higher level of interaction with family and friends, and health and time freedom. Still others live in parts of the world where, frankly speaking, the modus operandi is that of sheer poverty, where the daily grind is to provide a meal for the family.

It doesn't have to be that way. I have codified a simple method of coaching that anyone can do, regardless of his current circumstances. You see, in today's rapidly changing, fast-paced world, more and more people are desperately looking for help, step-by-step solutions, and a coach to guide them. That creates an incredible opportunity for people who are willing to implement simple yet powerful ways to meet those coaching needs.

Anyone can start a coaching business, anyone can coach, and anyone can live the life of his or her dreams as a result of effectively coaching others, no matter his background, his education, the country in which she lives, or her financial situation. Someone who has worked for someone else all of his life can build a coaching business. A stay-at-home mom who hasn't been employed outside the home in years can start a coaching business. A teenager who hasn't been to college can start a coaching business. A homeless person can start a coaching business. The poorest person in the poorest country in the world can start a coaching business. Someone with no expertise, no knowledge, and no money can start a coaching business, as long as she is willing to learn how to do it, and learn how to help the people she is coaching. And yet, the most educated person, with wide-ranging experience and knowledge, can also, if he so chooses, leave the corporate jungle and start a coaching business and create a new level of freedom in his life.

That's why I've written this book. My dream is to empower every person on earth to create a rewarding future, fulfilling expansive dreams and deep desires, while simultaneously enriching others by sharing experience and training.

And in the pages that follow, I show step-by-step exactly how to do just that. I show you how to create a rewarding future by building a simple coaching business that has at its core the premise that you are helping others do something you do well; that pays you well for helping others; and finally, that enables you to create for yourself a lifestyle based on financial and time freedom, so that you can live the rest of your life the way you desire!

Acknowledgements

In the course of becoming who I am, and in developing the coaching system I teach in this book, I've had numerous life experiences and relationships that have led me to the place of being able to share this system. Many wonderful people have influenced and guided me; multiple experiences and crises have tested, shaped, and molded me; and an almighty God who has a plan, not just for me, but for everyone else on earth, has empowered and directed me.

One of my guiding thoughts since teenage-hood has been the words of Paul the missionary in Philippians 4:13: "I can do all things through Christ which strengtheneth me." Those words have inspired me more times than I can count when I feel like I cannot go on; when my body wants to rest yet I drive it mercilessly to produce another page, another concept, another method of implementation; when my mind wants to slam on the brakes and rest and yet I force it to continue to think, to imagine, to weld into being the physical manifestation of my goals and visions.

Without the people who have influenced me, the experiences that have shaped me, the crises that have served as the catalyst for growth, and the successes that validate the hard work and harder mental effort, not only would this book not have been possible, but the concepts within it would never have been fleshed out in my life.

Although it would be impossible to list everyone who has influenced me over the years, I'll list those who have had the greatest impact.

My first mentors were unaware they were mentors: Robert Guay, John Simmons, George Sideris, John Scott, Mr. Glass, and Chuck and Carol Corson; their work ethic and mental perception formed a solid example for my current tenacity and my insight into human accomplishment.

Some of the people I learned the most from in developing my coaching system: Marlon Sanders, Jim Loehr, Tony Schwartz, Tellman Knudson, Harris Fellman, Ed Forteau, Kendall Summerhawk, Lisa Sasevich, JP Maroney, Kevin Nations, Milana Leshinsky, Christian Mickelsen, Ed Zimbardi, Timothy Ferris, Dan Kennedy, Russell Granger, Michael Masterson, and Yanik Silver. To all of you and all the others who have molded my growth process, I thank you from the bottom of my heart for your presence in my life. Without you this work wouldn't have been possible!

My Dad and his wife helped me in more ways than I can count, and most importantly cheered me on in an endeavor that could have just as easily failed.

My Mom instilled in me a strong work ethic and a confident mindset for which I shall always be grateful, and has steadfastly encouraged me to live a life of excellence and accomplishment.

My good friend Dave has been a source of relentless enthusiasm for my entrepreneurial dreams, endeavors, and achievements.

My four-legged friends, Cricket, Lily, Cookie, Willie, Wynona, Meika, Bert, Jake, Razzy, Dakota, and Pepper, who always listen when I share my dreams, concoct ways to accomplish those dreams, and torment myself when sometimes those methods don't work, have given me an incredible level of enjoyment over the last few years.

My wife Maryann has been a constant inspiration, a never-ending presence of love in my life who has afforded me the space and freedom to pursue the codification, development, and dissemination of my ideas about human potential and the implementation of systematic life and world improvement. Without her love and fire, this work would not be what it is today. Together, Maryann and Cricket give me reason to pause from my work to enjoy their presence and stay sane in the midst of trying to change the world! Maryann and Cricket, I love you both forever!

ANYONE CAN COACH

Transform Your Life
by Coaching Others to Excellence

Sean Mize

Chapter 1

You Can Coach

You have the inherent ability to show others how to do what you do well, to help them succeed, and to enrich both your life and theirs as you help them.

Anyone can coach. That's right. Anyone can coach—and so can you! Coaching is guiding others to do something more effectively, and you can do it, just like I have.

When I started my first online business, I wanted to share with others the skills that had enabled me to be successful, I wanted to earn a full-time income, and I wanted to have the flexibility and freedom to take time off and travel. I began by creating information products such as ebooks and audios, but I found that my clients were asking for more help than they could receive from books or home-study courses.

They wanted to be able to ask me questions personally, instead of just getting the information from books or audios. I couldn't meet all their needs by just creating more information products. That's when I launched a coaching program with core training and personal access to me.

My clients loved the instruction and the access to me, and I found that I loved the process. It was exciting to give my clients instruction and feedback, watch them implement it, and share the thrill of their results. I loved getting the email or phone call that said, "Thanks, Sean, for changing my life. I have looked long and hard for someone like you, and it's great to have found you."

I was hooked!

You see, until that point, I had been creating and selling information products to teach people my skills. But in most cases, information alone doesn't create results. Action, which includes implementation of the information, creates results. I found that clients who coached with me personally got much better results than clients who only purchased my training without a coaching element. Over time, as my coaching business grew, I developed and fine-tuned ways to deliver group coaching in such a way that group clients were able to obtain the same results as if they had worked with me one-on-one, while keeping my business ultra-simple and easy to run.

In the process, I've created a business that coaches others to success and opportunity while giving my family and me both financial and lifestyle freedom. My coaching business has created a passive income that allows us to take extended vacations, spend more time with family than we ever dreamed possible, and ski 30 + days a year.

YOU CAN CREATE A COACHING BUSINESS

The good news is, you can create a coaching business and lifestyle just like that, if you want. You can deliver and sell your coaching in an easy virtual format, without certifications, an office, or a fancy website. If you don't have a coaching business now, you can start from scratch; if you already have one, you can streamline it so that you can deliver your coaching 100% virtually—from home, a coffee shop, a beach in South America, a ski resort in Switzerland, or anywhere else in the world you want to work.

Perhaps you've been trying to find a way to leverage the internet to create not only an income stream, but a lifestyle based on time and geographic freedom. Maybe you want to be financially secure, work when and where you want, take time off for yourself and your family, and help others achieve a similar success. In the process of searching for a way to make your dream a reality, perhaps you've gotten stuck somewhere. Maybe you've tried to create and sell products, to sell other people's products, to sell traffic or advertising online, or you've tried some other popular method of building a business online, and you aren't getting the results you believe you deserve. But deep down inside, you know you could help others, if you could structure your knowledge and experience so that you could efficiently share it, and get paid for doing so.

With the Anyone Can Coach virtual coaching model, you can build a coaching business that is focused on helping others solve their problems or achieve their goals; that provides for you financially; and that allows you an incredible level of lifestyle freedom. And it's so easy to start a coaching business. Not only do you not need to start with a fancy website or extended education, you also don't need employees, a big team, or an office to work out of. You can start as small as you want, with as few as just one client; scale as big as you want, coaching as many clients as you choose; and build your business to fit your lifestyle and strengths perfectly. You aren't paid based on the number of hours you work; instead, you are paid based on the value of the results you can help your clients get, and based on how you choose to price your coaching. You don't report to a boss or a company; instead, you are responsible only to the needs of your clients. In short, a coaching business is not only a highly professional and highly paid business, but it is one of the easiest ways to start an online or home business.

Perhaps you are wondering, "how is this different from so many of the other coaching methods, coaching gyms, and membership models being taught online right now?" That's a great question! In fact, many of the other models can help you create a full-time business and financial freedom. However, one of my primary goals in developing and fine-tuning my Anyone Can Coach virtual coaching model was to design an ultra-simple way for someone to operate a coaching business in just a few hours a day, with an absolute minimum of extraneous emotional involvement and time commitment, rather than having a complicated business that requires a lot of time answering emails, keeping up with individual client's needs, and constantly scrambling to create new lessons and new offers.

A SIMPLE MODEL ANYONE CAN USE

This model is so simple that anyone can use it to get started in coaching, and yet it's robust and flexible so that experienced coaches can use it to streamline and simplify an existing coaching business to create the time and financial freedom about which they have dreamed. You can start building your coaching business from scratch, or begin simplifying your existing coaching business, right after reading this book, because coaching doesn't have to be complicated. It can be as simple as helping people do what you already know how to do, in an easy-to-implement structure that requires minimal time and energy from you. It might involve talking with your clients in a group mastermind-style session once a week, teaching them one new step to take each week, and giving them directions for implementing that new step. The following week you might check in with them and evaluate their progress with last week's step, and give them a new step to take. And you might encourage them to talk with and support each other between coaching calls.

Eventually, you'll find that you can automate much of the teaching delivery, and find yourself primarily in the role of motivating your clients as they study materials and implement action steps you have prepared long in advance. As a result of your automation, your clients get consistent results, and you can work less while helping more clients.

This book teaches you everything you need to know to create your own coaching business just like I've created mine. I've consolidated and streamlined every concept in such a way that you can immediately duplicate or imitate what I have done and create for yourself a life of success while helping others.

You'll find the exact methods I have used (and still use today) to sell and deliver coaching that gets my clients great results while allowing me to enjoy a life of financial freedom and personal satisfaction. I start by showing you how to define your coaching niche (what you will be helping people with), then I show you how to design and deliver your coaching program. I follow that with selling instructions—how to sell through personal consultation, group teleseminars, and sales letters—then I show you how to create a prospect-cultivating email campaign and how to get prospects to that email campaign and to your coaching offer. And finally, I give you some ideas for staying motivated, focused, and in control of your time, because no matter how much you learn, if you don't step out and do it . . . you won't get results!

You can use all the techniques and methods I teach in this book to create, deliver, and enroll clients in your own coaching program. You can do it if you are starting from scratch with no expertise. You can do it if you have expertise but don't know how to get the word out about your coaching program. And you can do it if you already have a coaching program but are frustrated because you are working too hard and getting burned out, or aren't able to enroll enough clients to make it worth your time financially. You really can create your own coaching program, deliver great coaching, empower your clients to new levels of success and achievement, and attain financial freedom for yourself, and in the following pages, I am going to show you how!

At the end of each chapter, I have included a list of key points and, where applicable, additional training sources or suggested reading to help you implement what you learn. And because I've found that sometimes my clients "get it" fastest when they see it done, as opposed to just being told how to do it, I've included examples or samples of steps you will do in building your business, such as emails to write, sample coaching program structures, and actual scripting for a sales call and a sales letter. I've also created a daily guided action plan and additional training resources, including more in-depth technical instructions for implementing things like recording coaching calls, delivering links and lessons, using autoresponders, uploading files, taking payments, etc., and have posted them at AnyoneCanCoach.net.

I challenge you to change your life today. You really can own your own online coaching business! You really can change people's lives through coaching. And if you already have a coaching business, you really can streamline your coaching delivery to allow you to work less and get paid more. You can change your life as you assist others in changing theirs.

I'm excited for you as you begin this journey!

Key Points

- You can coach. You can help others do things that come easily for you, but are difficult for them, and get paid for helping them.
- You can automate the delivery of your coaching so that you can easily work with multiple clients without creating additional stress or work for yourself.
- In this book, I show you step-by-step my complete system for creating a coaching business from scratch, or streamlining an existing coaching business, to create a lifestyle of efficiency and freedom.

Recommended Reading:

The 4-Hour Workweek: Escape 9-5, Live Anywhere, and Join the New Rich by Timothy Ferris

Get more at AnyoneCanCoach.net

<u>*Chapter 2*</u>

Choose How You Will Help Others

You can choose how you will help others, and become an expert in both niche knowledge and in the process of coaching others to achievement.

Inside each of us is the seed of accomplishment and purpose which contains the energy and raw materials for helping others change their lives. In order to effectively release the power of that seed and purpose so that you can impact others and the world, you need to know what that seed is, know the purpose for your life, and know how you can use it to best help others.

In the following pages, I'm going to share with you an exercise and some questions that I have found to be very useful in helping people determine where some of their natural skills lie, where perhaps they are naturally gifted or talented, and how they can best help others. If you know your purpose in life, but don't have clarity on how you can really help others, the exercise and questions will guide you to quickly identify how you can help others.

However, if you don't know your ultimate purpose in life —what you were created to accomplish and what you were specifically designed to do—even if you develop an understanding of your natural talents, you might find that you don't feel fulfilled, even when you are helping others in areas where you are naturally talented.

If that's the case, take the time to determine your true purpose in life. Once you know that, many times all the questions about how you can help others just melt away, because once you know your purpose, you simply act in accordance with that purpose, helping people the way you were designed to.

Take the time to discover your purpose, and to find out how you can personally impact the world. As a starting place, I recommend *The Purpose Driven Life*, by Rick Warren, which gives a spiritual perspective on finding your purpose. I have also found chapters 2 and 3 in *The Innovation Secrets of Steve Jobs*, by Carmine Gallo, to be highly insightful and offer a genuinely perceptive look into finding your passion and purpose based on the concept of following your heart and "finding your element."

YOU CAN LEARN TO COACH

In a few moments, I am going to share with you a simple exercise to help you identify your strengths and some of the possibilities of things you can help others with as a coach. As you are doing the following exercise to help you determine how you can really help people, and thus what might be a good area to coach in, realize that it is just that—an exercise to help you determine how you can best help others. It is only a guide. Be willing to think creatively about how can you help others. Are you good at listening? Are you good at working through challenges? Are you the kind of person who, when you hear of someone else's struggle, even if it is something you've never done before, has some level of clarity that makes you think, "is there an easy way to do that?"

If so, perhaps you have a natural leaning towards being able to help and coach others. If not, I'll be teaching you language and questioning patterns to make the process easier. All of those patterns are learnable, and will come easier as you start working with a few clients. No matter your experience, knowledge, or lack thereof, you can coach. You simply have to be willing to help people and choose something that interests you to form the first subject about which you will coach, and as you start helping people (aka coaching) you will find that you get clearer on exactly how you can help people. You see, at the beginning you may have to take some steps of faith, getting out and doing some things that are not 100% comfortable for you at first, trusting that over time they will become easier and more comfortable.

Remember when you first learned to drive, especially if you learned to drive on a manual transmission? The first 25 stoplights were probably embarrassing; you may have thought you were going to get hit because you kept stalling the car. But now, you probably don't consciously think about shifting gears when you drive. You might text message, eat a sandwich, talk with your kids, and think about your coaching business, all while your feet change gears on your car. It's really easy now. But if you hadn't been willing to spend the first 25 times you drove learning how, you still wouldn't be able to drive now. And coaching is like that. Anyone can coach. But it might not be easy the first time. Or maybe not even the 25th time. But if you stick with it, and genuinely want to help people, you can do it.

EXERCISE TO IDENTIFY YOUR STRENGTHS

List all of your life experiences. List your successes and your failures. Write down everything: personal challenges you have overcome, life problems you have solved, people problems you have worked out, crises you have survived, everything. Create a list of at least 25 successes, challenges, problems, and failures.

Here are some possible ideas:

You made it through adolescence.
You got your first job.

You have been promoted at work.

You have raised children.

You have raised teenagers.

You have started a business.

You have survived the death of a close family member.

You have survived the death of a close friend.

You have survived a nearly fatal car crash.

You have survived a divorce.

You have been married.

You have grown old healthily.

You have lost weight.

You have overcome an illness.

You have (fill in the blank).

Now create your own list, because this is about you. Start down the list and ask yourself which of the things you have overcome are challenges that others also struggle with. Which of these challenges would have gone easier for you if you had had someone who had "been there, done that" and could have given you some advice along the way? Which of these challenges would be easier for others to go through if they were to have access to your experience and guidance?

For example, if you've raised teenagers, you could probably offer a lot of advice to someone who is raising teenagers. If you have suffered the loss of a close family member, you could help others survive that as well. If you have ever been hired, you could offer advice to people looking for a job. If you have ever started a business, you could guide people in starting their own businesses. Just about anything you have done that was a struggle for you, is likely a struggle for other people. And if it's a struggle for other people, you can help them. That's what coaching is all about—helping people overcome their challenges and reach new heights by achieving their dreams and goals.

Another way that you can decide how you will help others is to think about what interests you. Ask yourself the following questions, perhaps writing down the answers, no matter how crazy they might feel, and see if a pattern emerges:

> If you could help others with anything in world, what would it be?
>
> What do you most like to help others with?
>
> Do people ever come to you for advice, and if so, what are the topics they come to you for advice on?
>
> If you could learn something new and share it with others, what would it be?
>
> If you could learn anything in the world and become an expert on it, what would it be?

Of course this is just a starting place for asking yourself what your interests are. Likely, deep down inside, you have some interests that perhaps you've never followed up on or learned about, and one of those interests might make a great coaching niche for you.

STRENGTHEN YOUR AREA OF EXPERTISE

Although you may have experiences, ideas, and solutions you can share with others, you may not have enough knowledge or expertise to feel comfortable coaching. You can change that by learning what you need to know to have the information and expertise your prospects are looking for.

You might purchase a few books that have been written on your topic. If you were to read 5–10 books on your topic, how would your level of knowledge change? How much more prepared would you be to help others?

You might purchase top-level training programs from other coaches online who teach the same thing or something similar to what you want to teach (or already teach). Imagine you were to study their programs, not just for the knowledge, but also for how the material is presented. How would your knowledge and expertise level change relative to where it is today?

You might find, after studying from multiple experts, that you now have more training and more knowledge than any one of your competitors. Once you have studied several experts in your niche and internalized the knowledge, you can restructure that internalized knowledge in a better, clearer, unique way that might give your clients a better experience and faster results than they would receive from your competition.

Another way to get started in a new niche where you don't have enough experience or knowledge is to interview other experts in that niche area. Imagine that you were to find 10 people that teach on the topic you want to teach on, interview each of them, and ask them questions that your clients might want the answers to. Within a very short period of time, you would likely develop a level of knowledge and expertise that might be better fitting for your clients than if they were to work with any one of those experts individually.

The ideas I have just shared with you can serve as a leaping-off point for you in quickly gaining the knowledge and expertise necessary to become an effective coach. You will find in working with your clients that if you don't know something, it is usually quite easy to find the answer for your client. And of course in finding that answer, you expand your own knowledge, and when another client asks the same question, you will know the answer.

COACHING OUTSIDE OF YOUR AREA OF EXPERTISE

What you coach someone to do can be something you know how to do well; however, you can also help people solve problems and get results you haven't personally experienced.

Perhaps you are a life coach and your client is going through something you haven't personally experienced. For example, perhaps your client is dealing with a problem with her teenage daughters and you've never dealt with that kind of problem. You can guide her through that experience by asking questions to help her understand her problem, showing her how to get the information she needs to solve her problem, and guiding her to implement that information so that she solves the problem.

Or perhaps someone has hired you to guide him through getting into graduate school. You may not personally know the steps required to get into graduate school, and in fact don't need to teach those steps. The steps themselves are likely readily available; possibly online, in a manual, or in a book. You or your client can easily access the information itself. The problem for your client, however, likely isn't the information itself; it is likely the implementation of that information. He needs you to hold him accountable for doing the steps, to motivate him when he gets stuck on a step, or to give him ideas or guidance when he doesn't understand something. You don't necessarily have to be an expert in what you are coaching, but you do need to have an understanding of how to get someone to take action on what he knows, or to take action to find out what he doesn't know.

I'm not suggesting that you blindly go into coaching something you don't know anything about. In fact, just the opposite: I'm suggesting you find creative ways to learn the information. But don't allow an incomplete knowledge to hold you back from getting started. It will take time to enroll your first few clients, and you can simultaneously become more experienced and knowledgeable while you are building your coaching business. You can start by coaching clients at lower levels (and at lower prices) and as you learn more, you can coach at higher, more advanced levels (and charge higher prices).

Key Points

- To help decide what to coach, think about t
you've accomplished or survived with whi
could help others.
- Be willing to study and research to learn
about helping others, and to become an
the area in which you choose to coach.
- The primary goal in your coaching busin
be to help others, not "to make money." However,
you focus on helping others, the money will follow.

Recommended Reading:

The Purpose Driven Life by Rick Warren

The Innovation Secrets of Steve Jobs by Carmine Gallo

Get more at AnyoneCanCoach.net

Chapter 3

Design and Deliver

Create a coaching curriculum that guides your clients to achieving their goals, and deliver your coaching through targeted instruction and client interaction.

CREATE A MASTER OUTLINE OF YOUR COACHING FOCUS

The first step in designing your coaching program is to create a master outline of what you can help people with. Write out each of the topics you can teach on or help people with. For example, if your niche is health coaching, your topics might be:

1. Basic Concepts of Healthy Living
2. Importance of Exercise
3. Importance of Food
4. Importance of Stress Management
5. Social Relationships and Their Impact on Health
6. Weight Management
7. Disease Management

8. Lifestyle Management
9. Supplementation
10. Tying it All Together

In this example, there are 10 topics. You can have more or less than 10, but something close to 10 is usually the easiest to work with.

Next, create a list of sub-topics for each of the topics. For example, under the topic "Importance of Food," you might list each of the types of food you will be discussing:

Vegetables
Fruit
Meats
Dairy
Grains
Empty Calories (e.g., sugar)
Seeds
Oils
Spices
Fiber

Assuming you end up with 10 topics and 10 sub-topics per topic, you would have a total of 100 sub-topics.

I call this a 10 x 10 matrix. Obviously if you have 12 topics and 8 sub-topics each, you would have a 12 x 8 matrix. You don't need to have the same number of sub-topics for each topic, but all together the closer you can get to 100 subtopics in total, the easier it will be to create coaching lessons and future products.

You can use this matrix as an outline for your coaching program lessons, and as a master guide for planning future books, home-study courses, an online content campaign, and an email campaign.

DETERMINE THE LENGTH OF YOUR COACHING PROGRAM

How long should your coaching program be? For example, should it be a 13-week program, a 6-month program, a year-long program, or an open-ended monthly program?

Although this will vary from client to client based on each client's needs, and from niche to niche based on the time it might take to comfortably teach each client what she needs to know to achieve her goals, here are two key questions to help you determine the optimal length of your coaching program:

1. How long will it take you to help someone achieve an initial goal or result?

2. How long will it take you to help someone achieve a long-term goal or result?

You might find that the first question is answered with 13 weeks or 6 months, and that the second question is answered with 12 months or 2 years.

Of course, there are a few factors at play here. One is the definition of the client's goals. More in-depth or larger goals will take longer to achieve. Because this is coaching, you will be doing more than just teaching the information; you will be working with the client so he is able to implement the teachings and achieve tangible or measurable results. For many of your clients, their challenges have been developing for months or years, and it is rare that you can completely solve their problems and get them on a sustainable path in a short time. Therefore, you must be careful that you don't underestimate the time it will take to really help someone.

Some clients might want to hire you initially to help them achieve complete mastery of their challenges; others might like to "try you out" on a portion of their goals initially, then hire you to help them go the rest of the way after the initial coaching.

Because of this, it is often advantageous to offer at least two coaching programs: one that helps people achieve some milestone in the journey towards their long-term goals, and another that offers a higher level of achievement.

You might offer an initial program for 13 weeks or 6 months, and a higher-level program for 12–24 months or more. You could also have multiple entry-level 13-week or 6-month programs, one for each primary area that you help people with, each of which could serve as a stepping stone to enrolling in your "complete" or higher-level program.

WHY GROUP COACHING INSTEAD OF ONE-ON-ONE?

Group coaching allows you to help more people simultaneously, it allows your clients to get a more standardized (and therefore more consistently complete) experience, and it gives your clients the benefit of masterminding with each other in addition to getting instruction from you.

Although most of your clients will have individual needs based on their unique situations and circumstances, their core needs will be similar; you'll be teaching all your clients the same core concepts, with slight modifications for each client based on his unique needs. Those slight modifications tend to be only about 5–10% of the total teaching you do, meaning that for every hour you spend teaching the average client, only 3–6 minutes is spent on the slight modifications and customizations for his needs. The rest of the time is spent teaching the same things you are teaching your other clients, so with one-on-one coaching, you are repeatedly teaching the same core material. However, with group coaching, you teach all your clients the core concepts simultaneously, and only work with each client individually on the slight modifications and customizations for his specific needs.

Because you are using recorded training for your lessons over the long run, all your clients get identical training on each topic, as opposed to delivering the training live for each individual client, in which case the experience changes from day to day depending on your energy level and mental acuity on that day. Clients are also able to study the lesson material when it is convenient for them, instead of being committed to you at a specific time. And if someone misses a live group call, it's okay; because you record each group coaching call, he can listen to the recording after the call.

Additionally, as clients participate on the group coaching call, a mastermind effect occurs. One client will ask a question, and as you answer her question, other clients get ideas they can use, but would not have thought of if they weren't on the group call. They also have the chance to mastermind with other clients in the coaching program.

In summary, with group coaching, you can help more clients achieve their goals, and you can work fewer hours while making more money; with one-on-one coaching, the number of clients you can help, and the income you can earn, is limited by the number of hours you can work, because you can only work with (and charge) one client at a time.

Here's a numerical example to illustrate this: Let's imagine that you charge $100 an hour for your time, and that you can actively coach for 15 hours a week (if you actively coach much more than that, you will likely burn out quickly). This means that your maximum coaching income is $1,500 a week, and that you can work with a maximum of 15 people per week, which limits both your income and the number of people you can help.

Now let's imagine that instead of charging by the hour, you charge based on the results someone can achieve by working with you. Let's say that instead of charging each client $100 an hour for, say, 10 hours of one-on-one coaching, for a total of $1,000, you charge each client $1,000 based on the results that client could get by working with you one-on-one for 10 hours. However, instead of working with each client one-on-one for 10 hours, you work with multiple clients together as a group for 20 hours, achieving the same results in each client's life as if you had worked one-on-one with him for 10 hours.

Because you can work with a larger number of clients simultaneously, you end up earning much more per hour. In this example, imagine you enroll 20 clients at $1,000 each, for a total of $20,000, working with them as a group for 20 hours. Because you are working with more people at one time, you will make $1,000 an hour, instead of $100 an hour. If you were to enroll and work with 100 clients simultaneously, your revenue would be $100,000 for the same 20 hours worked, yielding $5,000 an hour to you. Because your clients are getting the same level of results as working with you individually, the price continues to be fair to them, but you earn significantly more per hour, and you can help many more people without burning out or running out of time.

DELIVER ONE-ON-ONE COACHING

When you are first starting out, if you don't have enough prospects to justify offering a group coaching program, you can start out with one-on-one clients, then transition over time to coaching groups of clients.

In your first coaching session with a new one-on-one client, determine what she wants to achieve, and create a step-by-step plan with estimated time frames for achieving each goal or milestone. This time-based implementation schedule will serve as a guide to what you work on in your coaching sessions.

To create the step-by-step plan, assemble all the topics you need to teach, based on what your client needs and what she has expressed she wants to learn. Once you have gathered these topics together, place them in a logical order for presenting the material. Assign a time value to each component based on how long you think you'll need to teach each component. Here is an example of what this schedule might look like:

Week 1: Overview; set expectations
Week 2: Skill 1—30 minutes; Skill 2—30 minutes
Week 3: Skill 2—1 hour
Week 4: Skill 2—30 minutes; Skill 3—45 minutes
Week 5: Skill 4—45 minutes
Week 6: Skill 4—45 minutes

Week 7: Skill 5—1 hour
Week 8: Skill 5—1 hour
Week 9: Skill 5—1 hour
Week 10: Skill 6—1 hour
Week 11: Skill 6—1 hour
Week 12: Review and wrap up

Once you have this implementation schedule in place, it makes it easy to know what you will work on each time you meet. You will teach on the next topic based on the schedule you have created, and evaluate your client's progress on the prior step. Here is a typical flow of a coaching session:

1. Opening—small talk, etc.
2. Give directions for doing the next step.
3. Give a homework assignment or instructions for the week.
4. Evaluate progress from the prior week. Ask questions like: "What have you accomplished since we last talked?" and "Do you have any questions about anything we've worked on?"

When you follow this model of creating and implementing a step-by-step plan for achieving a certain result, your clients can systematically achieve results. From time to time you may need to slow down or speed up, or make adjustments or changes to the game plan, but over time as you lead clients through the steps necessary to achieve their goals, they will be able to get the results they desire.

No matter how firmly you try to adhere to the schedule, your clients will move faster than you expect some weeks, and slower other weeks. If you try to force a certain amount of learning or action each week, you and your clients will quickly get frustrated. If a particular concept or implementation step takes longer than expected, spend more time on that component than initially outlined. If it moves faster than expected, you can move to the next component sooner.

Record all the training you do with your one-on-one clients. When you enroll your initial one-on-one coaching clients, you can offer a discount in exchange for your clients' permission to record their lessons and use these with future clients. Once you've taught on a particular topic and recorded it, when it is time to work on that topic with another client, you can give him the recorded session to listen to and study first. When you meet for your coaching time, you can focus on specific implementation ideas instead of teaching the core material.

GROUP COACHING

Group your clients according to similar needs, so although the implementation of your techniques or advice may vary from client to client, they all receive the same information and training as if they were coaching with you one-on-one.

Send group clients an email before the first coaching call, asking them specific questions to determine exactly what they want to work on and achieve over the course of the coaching term. This allows you to begin coaching on the first call, rather than spending the time as a group determining what everyone wants to work on (when you use a live group call to speak with everyone about what they want to work on, some clients don't participate so the results of the discussion are skewed, and the clients who don't participate often feel excluded).

Once you have the goals from all or most of the clients in your coaching program, create a step-by-step schedule of what you are going to cover and in what order, in much the same way as you prepare the working outline for a one-on-one client, for example:

Week 1: Overview; set expectations
Week 2: Skill 1—30 minutes; Skill 2—30 minutes
Week 3: Skill 2—1 hour
Week 4: Skill 2—30 minutes; Skill 3—45 minutes
Week 5: Skill 4—45 minutes
Week 6: Skill 4—45 minutes
Week 7: Skill 5—1 hour
Week 8: Skill 5—1 hour

Week 9: Skill 5—1 hour
Week 10: Skill 6—1 hour
Week 11: Skill 6—1 hour
Week 12: Review and wrap up

The delivery of the group coaching call will also operate very similarly to the one-on-one coaching call:

1. Opening—small talk, etc.
2. Give directions for doing the next step.
3. Give a homework assignment or instructions for the week.
4. Evaluate progress from the prior week. Ask questions like: "What have you accomplished since we last talked?" and "Do you have any questions about anything we've worked on?"

As you do with a one-on-one call, record all sessions. With the group call, an added advantage to recording the call is that if someone can't make one of the calls, he only misses out on the live interaction. He can listen to the training material on his own later. As with recording one-on-one coaching calls, this allows you to easily use these recorded lessons as the core material for future coaching programs.

DELIVER RECORDING AND HOMEWORK ASSIGNMENT

Use an audio conference call (teleseminar) service to deliver your coaching. I've listed a few choices here: recommendedteleseminars.com. When choosing a teleseminar service, focus on reliability, the ability to easily record, and easy backup access to the recordings.

Once you have completed the coaching call, upload the recording of the call to your server or web host, or use the storage solution from the conference call service. Put a link to the recording in a pdf document (you can easily create one by using the "save or export as a pdf" option in your word processor or by using acrobat.com/createpdf), along with links to any relevant resources you may have mentioned during the call, and include written directions for completing the homework in the pdf document.

Then upload the pdf document to your web host or server, put a link to the pdf document in an autoresponder email (or attach the pdf to the email), and send the email to your coaching clients using your chosen autoresponder service. In this way, your clients have easy access to the recording, relevant links, and the homework assignment. You will also have a pdf document with all the lesson materials which you can use for lesson delivery to future classes. (For more detailed technical instructions for creating the recordings, creating pdfs, creating links, uploading and storing files, etc., go to AnyoneCanCoach.net.)

DELIVER COACHING BASED ON PRE-RECORDED LESSONS

Once you have recorded a series of coaching calls, you can deliver your training to future clients by using your autoresponder service to send the recorded lessons to your clients, rather than teaching the lesson material live on the coaching calls. All live coaching time can then be used for questions, discussion, and individualized instruction based on the recorded core material.

This allows you to send the first lesson to each client when he enrolls, and to use the autoresponder to send future lessons based on a predetermined timing (for example, one lesson every 2 weeks). Because your clients receive recorded core training, you can have them all attend your live Q&A coaching calls, regardless of the particular lesson each client is individually studying at the time of the call.

TRANSITION FROM ONE-ON-ONE TO GROUP COACHING

Once you have at least 5 one-on-one clients, you can offer all of them unlimited access to your group coaching, at no additional charge, with one requirement: they must each be willing to come to every group coaching call and actively participate on each call.

This is a win-win scenario, because your one-on-one clients receive significantly more access to you at no additional charge, and your group coaching call is pre-populated with clients. For example, if you have 5 one-on-one clients who have all agreed to participate in the group calls, when you enroll your first group client, he won't be the only client on the group call. And as you enroll additional clients, the size of the group will be self-perpetuating. Over time, as earlier-enrolled clients drop out or become less active, you will enroll new clients who fill the gap, and your group coaching program develops a sense of continuity.

Although I personally prefer giving group access to one-on-one clients to create a starter group, as I've described above, an easy way to get started without one-on-one clients is to offer low-cost or even free charter memberships to an initial group of 5–10 clients, with the requirement that they all actively participate in the group coaching calls..

UPGRADE YOUR COACHING CLIENTS

When your clients complete a specific coaching program, or when they outgrow the coaching program in which they are enrolled, you can upgrade them to a higher-level or longer-term coaching program. For example, perhaps a client initially enrolls in your entry-level 13-week coaching program. Near the end of the term, you can offer her access to another coaching program. This might be another 13-week coaching program on a different topic or at a different level, or this might be a longer term coaching program such as a 6-month, one-year, or ongoing monthly-participation program.

SAMPLE COACHING PROGRAM STRUCTURES

Here are a few examples of how you could structure your coaching program:

12-Week Coaching Program:

Weekly live group calls
45 minutes of teaching each week
Homework assignment each week
Email access to you
Each week's call recorded and sent to clients

6-Month Coaching Program:

2 group coaching calls per month
45 minutes of teaching each week
Homework assignment each week
Monthly 20-minute one-on-one consultation with you
Lessons recorded for future use
Short pdf lessons for weeks between group calls

Long-Term Coaching Program:

2 group coaching calls per month (q and a based)
Pre-recorded lessons used for core training
2 homework assignments per month via pdf
Email access to you

You can mix and match the length of the program, how many times you meet each month, the type of access (e.g., group, one-on-one, or email access), how you deliver the lessons and the homework assignments, and how you hold clients accountable for doing the work.

ADDITIONAL COACHING PROGRAM COMPONENTS

Although I generally recommend group telephone coaching, autoresponder lesson delivery, and feedback and accountability on a live group coaching call as a simple coaching model that is easy to deliver, provides great consistent teaching, and gives your clients personal access to you, the list on the following pages will give you some mix-and-match ideas you can use to customize your coaching program.

MIX-AND-MATCH OPTIONS TO USE TO CUSTOMIZE YOUR COACHING PROGRAM

Teaching core (how you deliver the actual lessons or learning materials):

- Audio—(live telephone or pre-recorded)
- Video—(live webinar or pre-recorded)
- Reports—pdf delivery
- Books
- Done-for-you elements (sales pages, services, marketing, articles, newsletters, etc.)
- Look-over-your-shoulder opportunities (watch you work live on video, templates of your process, etc.)
- Contests
- Weekly or monthly faxes
- Newsletter
- Private membership site
- Autoresponder
- Niche-specific software or technology
- Monthly-topic teleseminar
- Physical CDs, transcripts, manuals, etc.
- Articles about clients
- Interviews with clients
- Forms, templates, manuals

Coaching core (how you give feedback and answer questions):

- Email coaching
- Instant messenger coaching
- Telephone coaching
- Live teleseminar (audio) coaching
- Live webinar (video) coaching

Accountability core (gives a client the ability to hold himself accountable by creating regular updates of his progress):

- Daily progress emails
- Weekly progress emails
- Monthly progress emails
- Daily progress report (word processing doc or spreadsheet)
- Weekly progress report (word processing doc or spreadsheet)
- Monthly progress report (word processing doc or spreadsheet)
- Telephone call
- Webinar

Homework element (instructions to perform activities that will lead to desired results in coaching program):

- Email the homework assignment
- Pdf (tutorial-based instruction)
- Verbally give the homework assignment on the coaching call
- Record the homework assignment on an audio
- Record the homework assignment on a video

Key Points

- Create a master outline of what your clients want to accomplish, and use it as a roadmap and planning guide for your coaching program.
- Use one-on-one coaching sparingly; focus on building your coaching practice based on group coaching for efficiency and best results.
- Deliver coaching using telephone conferencing and record all sessions for future use.
- Upgrade coaching clients to higher levels of coaching over time.

Additional Training:

howtosellcoachingprograms.com

Technology Resources:

AnyoneCanCoach.net
recommendedteleseminars.com.
recommendedautoresponders.com

Get more at AnyoneCanCoach.net

Chapter 4

Language to Use to Coach Clients

Although your coaching shouldn't be scripted, there are question patterns that work well for facilitating change in your clients' lives.

Although there are no exact special words that you should be using in your coaching to get specific results, there are types of questions and questioning patterns that can help you help your clients get the results they desire. When you use these questions, you can often very quickly get to the root of the matter in their lives or situations, and when you do that, people tend to get results. They get the results because once they realize what is holding them back, they realize what they are missing, or they realize what the solution is, they often just take the next step and do the action required to get the result they are seeking.

In the next few pages, I am going to share with you some of the questions I use with my clients that help me get the best results. I'll be giving you a wide range of questions you can use to get results in many different scenarios.

The goal with coaching is to get results for your clients by leading your clients down a path through which they get results for themselves. You see, you aren't actually getting the results in your clients' lives; instead, they are getting their own results. You are the facilitator. You are the person who holds them accountable. But your clients are the ones who actually do the work that results in change. And because each client is different in the way that his mind works, different questions will yield different results with different clients.

Although the exact questions you will use in each different scenario will vary, the general pattern will be to identify the problem, determine what it means for someone to continue to have the problem, what it would mean to get rid of the problem, and then propose (or lead the client to identify for himself) a solution. By using this process of asking questions to identify not only the problem, but the result of the problem and what it would mean to get rid of the problem and find a solution, the client becomes emotionally involved in realizing the impact of continuing to live with the problem or challenge, and she becomes emotionally involved in finding and implementing the solution. Because of the emotional involvement, it becomes easier for someone to follow through on making the change. You see, as humans, we tend to place a higher value on what we emotionally understand, or on what is emotionally impactful for us. When we only use logic to guide someone to making change, once the initial excitement over making the change wears off, he tends to fall away from implementing the solution and making real change occur. But when emotion is anchored to not just the pain of not solving the problem, but to the end result that will occur after doing the work to solve the problem, the client has a deeper internal level of commitment and desire to see the problem through to a solution.

Because I want you to get an intuitive feel for how these coaching questions work, so that you can intuitively ask them in a way that leads your client to become emotionally involved in the process of making change, I am going to give you several examples of questions, question patterns, and thorough processes to use. And rather than give them to you in a step-by-step, use-this-first—use-this-second manner, which may lead you to fall into a habit of moving through these questions formulaically instead of intuitively, based on each individual client's needs and responsiveness, I am going to give them to you as groups of questions that lead to a particular emotional response. As you read through them, you will begin to see some common patterns, and get an intuitive feel for how the questioning process will work.

I'll give you the questions, then comment on them and give some examples of common coaching scenarios in which I ask questions and carry on a dialogue with a hypothetical client. Use these scenarios as examples and to stimulate your thought process about working with clients, rather than as a scripted guide to working with specific scenarios.

Here are some questions you can use in your coaching:

What exactly do you want to accomplish?

What exactly do you want to accomplish in the next 3–6 months?

What do you want to accomplish in the next 30 days?

What do you want to accomplish this week?

What is the next step?

What do you think is holding you back?

Why did you struggle with that last week?

What could you change this week to get this done?

I wonder if you could . . .

Let's think about this . . . what if you . . . ?

Let's brainstorm for a minute. We'll both put some ideas down, then go from there. How does that sound?

How about . . . ? What do you think?

What do you think about . . . ?

How about if you did . . . ?

Maybe you could . . . ?

Imagine if you did . . . ?

Let's set a schedule for this week.

What if you were to accomplish (some goal) this week?

How about . . . ?

Some questions for using in a group:

Does what I just shared with (Name of Client) resonate with anyone else?

Is that something you could apply in your own situation?

What if we altered it just a little, is that something that would help you?

Let's dig a little deeper into these questions:

So what exactly do you want to accomplish?

That can be based on a time frame, for example:

What exactly do you want to accomplish in the next 3-6 months?

Or:

What do you want to accomplish in the next 30 days?

You can ask a variation of that question each time you meet with your client; for example, with a weekly-access client, you might ask:

So what do you want to accomplish this week?

Once someone has started working on his long-term plan and he knows what the steps are, when you ask that question it allows him to think about what he needs to do this week to get closer to his goal. And often once he has that clarification, he simply does the next step. But if you don't ask the question, he doesn't think about what is next, so he doesn't do it.

Here's another question:

What is the next step?

Many times someone knows what the next step is, but she just hasn't done it yet. When you ask this question, she will tell you what the next step is; then you can ask her if she wants to do that step this week. She says, "*yes*." She does it.

I know this seems so simple, and yet this is how people get results. It is a bit like hiring a personal trainer if you are trying to lose weight. You know how to lose weight. Eat less, move more, right? But we all have trouble doing it, don't we? So what good is a personal trainer? The biggest thing is knowing that he will be at the gym at 6:00 whether we are there or not. And we will be embarrassed if we don't show up. So we get up, go, laugh a little, work a little—and in 6 months we feel better. Same thing with coaching. People need the regular guidance, and that is the single biggest thing they are paying you for.

In fact, I have discovered that sometimes the less you teach when you coach, the more results you get. Just teach clients what they need to know to do the next step. Most people can't do 5 things at one time, so don't push it. Even if you can. Give them one thing at a time. Let them complete each step before giving the next one. Sure, it may feel slower in the short term, but in the long run, clients get better results. And results are what it is all about.

Here are some more questions:

What do you think is holding you back?

Why did you struggle with that last week?

What could you change this week to get this done?

Notice I'm not giving advice; I'm letting the client tell me what she needs to do next. She usually knows. When she doesn't, you can offer advice or give instructions. When you give advice or instructions, sometimes if you position the advice as an idea or a thought and let your client come to the final conclusion, she can get better results. The reason is that if someone feels that she has thought of it herself, she takes greater ownership of the next step, and she is more likely to take action on it.

The way to do this is with statements or questions like these:

I wonder if you could . . .

Let's think about this . . . what if you . . . ?

Let's brainstorm for a minute. We'll both put some ideas down, then go from there. How does that sound?

How about . . . ? What do you think?

Once you ask, wait. Don't say anything. Even if it's 2 minutes. It may feel like a really long time. It's okay. Let your client come up with the next thing. The more involved your client is, the more action she will take.

Here are some more phrases I use:

What do you think about . . . ?

How about if you did . . . ?

Maybe you could . . . ?

Imagine if you did . . . ?

Let's set a schedule for this week.

What if you were to accomplish (some goal) this week?

How about . . . ?

Notice these are all leading questions or statements. They are designed to lead your client to coming up with the necessary conclusion to get results.

Here are some more examples of questions you can use:

Imagine if you were to think about it this way (give an example relevant to the client's scenario).

Could you think about . . . ?

What if you were to imagine . . . ?

Have you ever thought about . . . ?

Here is an example of a pattern you can use when helping a client work through a challenge:

So, how is that challenge affecting you?

What kind of results are you not getting (or losing out on) as a result of that challenge?

How much longer are you willing to allow that challenge to exist?

So let me ask you this, are you willing to overcome this challenge?

What would it really mean, deep down inside, to overcome this challenge?

Are you ready to tackle this challenge?

So what do you see as the first step?

What do you think the next step would be?

How long do you think this process might take?

What would be the end result of following through on this?

How would that feel?

Would it be worth it?

Are you ready to just do it?

Notice how I am intentionally leading someone down a path of not just deciding to change, but also of determining the steps necessary and identifying the end result and the feelings associated with that end result. I believe it is important to anchor the long-term result to a feeling or a set of feelings that can remain as an emotional driver to serve as motivation to stick with making the change.

These questions also work great in a group environment. If you work with one person on something for 5 or 10 minutes on a group call, when you have finished working with that client, ask something like this to the entire group:

> *Does what I just shared with (Name of Client) resonate with anyone else?*

> Or:

> *Is that something you could apply in your own situation?*

> *What if we altered it just a little, is that something that would help you?*

This allows you to really draw in the other clients on the call, and get them to actively participate in the learning, even when you are working with one person personally on the group call.

Obviously these are only a small fraction of the number of different questions and variations of questions that you can ask to get action from your clients. The key is in asking questions that get your clients to think about the answer, formulate an answer, and then agree to take action on the next step. Over time, you will know which clients can get more done each week or month. Only give someone as much direction as that person can implement in the given time period. It is usually better to give someone a small goal and have him accomplish it, than to give him a big goal and have him do half. Very few people are motivated by setting unrealistic goals and realizing that although they likely won't achieve the unrealistic goal, they will achieve more than if they would have set a smaller goal. I am personally motivated by setting bigger goals than I can reasonably achieve in a given time frame, and perhaps you are too; but realize that most of your clients are probably not motivated well that way. The purpose of your coaching is for your clients to get results, and your job as coach is to maximize the likelihood that your clients will achieve what they set out to achieve.

Of course, having said that, your job is to do your best. Not everyone will implement everything you teach or coach, no matter how well you teach it or coach it. And the actual implementation is not your responsibility. Your responsibility is to create the best framework possible for your clients to get results, but it is each client's personal responsibility to actually do the work and get the results.

Now that I've shared with you some questioning patterns you can use with your clients, I'll give you a few examples of specific coaching scenarios:

Client is trying to determine what is holding him back from success in his home business:

You:

"So what is holding you back?"

Client:

"I'm not sure, I feel like I keep trying to do different things, but none of them is getting me the results I am looking for."

You:

"What have you tried?"

Client:

"I have tried (names things he has tried)."

You:

"What happened when you tried (the first thing)?"

Client:

(tells story, this happened, that happened, etc.)

You:

"So what do you think went wrong?"

Client:

"I think it was (names problems)."

You:

"What could you have done differently?"

Client:

(names things he could have done differently)

You:

"What happened when you tried (the second thing)?"

Client:

(tells story, this happened, that happened, etc.)

You:

"So what do you think went wrong?"

Client:

"I think it was (names problems)."

You:

"What could you have done differently?"

Client:

(names things he could have done differently)

You:

"What happened when you tried (the third thing)?"

Client:

(tells story, this happened, that happened, etc.)

You:

"So what do you think went wrong?"

Client:

"I think it was (names problems)."

You:

"What could you have done differently?"

Client:

(names things he could have done differently)

You:

"Are you beginning to see a pattern here as we are talking about what didn't work?"

Client:

"Yes, I think I am; wow, what wonderful clarity."

You:

"So what do you think you could have done differently all together?"

Client:

(names things)

You:

"Would it be worth it to you to make those changes?"

Client:

"Yes, of course"

You:

"So which of those changes do you want to start with this week?"

Notice in this example, I haven't taught the client anything. Of course, I would if necessary. But it often isn't. I am simply asking questions which lead the client to make a discovery he can follow through on. If someone feels as though he is part of the discovery process, he often feels as though he owns the solution. And if he feels like he owns the solution, he is more likely to take the steps to make the change. And if he takes the steps to make the change, he will get more results than if he is simply told what to do and then doesn't do it.

One of the biggest predictors about whether or not your coaching will get results for your clients is how involved your clients are in owning their solutions. Your coaching process must draw out client ownership of solutions in order to generate the highest level of results.

Here's another example:

Client is trying to determine what is holding her back from achieving a promotion at work:

You:

"So what is holding you back from achieving that promotion?"

Client:

(gives one reason)

You:

"What else is holding you back?"

Client:

(gives another thing that is holding her back)

You:

"What else?"

Client:

(shares something else)

You:

"Is there anything else?"

Client:

"No, I think that is about it."

Note: so far you have aided the client in identifying the problems; next, you will get the client to realize what those problems mean for her and what it would mean for her to solve those problems.

You:

"So how does it feel, allowing these problems to hold you back?"

Client:

"It doesn't feel good; it feels like (names how she feels)."

You:

"So how much longer are you willing to feel that way?"

Client:

"Not any longer. I am tired of feeling this way."

You:

"So what's it going to take to make this a real change, instead of just trying to attack these problems each week unsuccessfully?"

Client:

(gives ideas)

You:

"So what would be the result of making those changes?"

Client:

"I would experience (names the results)."

You:

"So how would that feel?"

Client:

(tells you how it would feel)

You:

"Would it be worth it?"

Client:

"Yes, of course, it would be great."

You:

"But up until now, you always stop short of the final result. How is this time going to be different?"

Client:

(tells you)

You:

"Are you really ready to make this change?"

Client:

"Yes, absolutely, let's do it!"

At this point, you have the complete buy-in of the client to making this change happen. You can now create a time-based schedule for achieving the goal.

The conversation I've just described is similar to one you can have regarding individual weekly action. Perhaps a client is experiencing frustration in a particular step; the same types of questions can identify what is going wrong so it can be fixed, and can elicit the emotional response necessary to spur the long-term change.

As you can see, the pattern for dealing with any change is very similar: ask questions to identify the problem, find out how that problem is impacting someone, what it means to solve the problem, and what someone is willing to do to achieve mastery over the problem. This can be done at any level of problem solving. For example, this can be done with one-year or 10-year challenges. This can be done with small problems that may take a few weeks or months to solve, or bigger problems that may take a year or more to solve. And it can be done with each individual roadblock that comes up in the implementation of dealing with the bigger challenges.

Here is another example:

Client is trying to make a change to her diet:

You:

"So what is going on with your diet right now?"

Client:

(tells you)

You:

"So what is the result of that diet?"

Client:

(tells you)

You:

"What do you not like about that result?"

Client:

(tells you)

You:

"How much longer are you willing to continue to get that (bad) result?"

Client:

(tells you)

You:

"On a scale of 1 to 10, with 10 being very strong, how committed are you to making this change?"

Client:

"I would say I am about a '7.'"

You:

"So tell me about that, what does it mean to be a '7' to you, what does that really mean?"

Client:

(tells you)

You:

"What is it going to take to get you to a '9' or a '10'?"

Client:

(tells you)

You:

"What would it mean for you to get to a '9' or a '10'?"

Client:

(tells you)

You:

"What would be the end result of that?"

Client:

(tells you)

You:

"Obviously that is going to be a lot of work over time. How committed are you to making that change?"

Client:

(tells you)

You:

"Are you ready to make that change?"

Client:

"Yes, that's why I am working with you."

You:

"Excellent, what do you think the first step should be?"

Notice that once you have gotten the client to explain why she is ready to make the change or solve the problem, you are going to involve her in the change-making process, rather than just telling her what to do and how to do it. Of course, if you get to something she doesn't know how to do, or she misses a step as you go through this process, you are going to suggest or give her that step or steps.

Continuing:

Client:

(offers suggestion for the first step)

You:

"So what is the next step?"

Client:

(offers suggestion for the next step)

You:

"And what about the next step?"

Client:

(tells you)

You:

"Is there another step?"

Client:

"No, I think that's all."

You:

"OK, what about (something that could be a step), do you think you should add that in?"

Client:

"OK, that might work as well."

You:

"Why do you think you should add that step in?"

Client:

(tells you)

Notice that because you have given her the step and you want her to own this step for herself just as if she had suggested it, you are asking a why-question to get her emotionally involved in this step as well. Of course, you could also do that with the steps she suggested; for example, by asking her, "why do you think that is important?" or "why do you want to include that step?"

Continuing:

You:

"So now that you have these steps, what is it going to mean to you to implement these steps?"

Client:

(tells you)

You:

"Is it going to be worth the effort to do this work?"

Client:

(tells you)

You:

"Why?"

Client:

(tells you)

You:

"How is it going to feel for you to accomplish all of this?"

Client:

(tells you)

You:

"Excellent, well let's do this: let's set up an implementation schedule for making all of this happen."

And of course at this point you'll help her put together an implementation schedule for the steps you have agreed upon. The following week, you will ask her what she has accomplished and how it feels to accomplish it, continuing to reinforce the emotional element in achieving the change in her life.

At this point, I've given you several examples of how this works, and by now you are probably seeing the similarities in the process, although the exact questions may change based on the exact scenario. Imagine I were to give you more sample scenarios, for example:

Client is trying to make a relationship change:

Ask about what is going wrong in the relationship. Find out how it is impacting her that it is going wrong, how it would feel to make the change, and how important it is to her to make the change. Then ask what the next step is.

Client is trying to get rid of a bad habit in her business:

Ask about what is going wrong in the business. Find out how it is impacting her that it is going wrong, how it would feel to make the change, and how important it is to her to make the change. Then ask what the next step is.

Client is trying to increase the productivity of her workers or contractors:

Ask about what is going wrong. Find out how it is impacting her that it is going wrong, how it would feel to make the change, and how important it is to her to make the change. Then ask what the next step is.

CONCLUDING THOUGHTS ABOUT THE COACHING PROCESS

It would probably be beneficial to go back and read through the questions and question patterns from time to time. In fact, when you first start coaching, if you were to spend 5 minutes before each coaching session reading through the questions in this chapter, you would likely find that questions come more easily to you on the call. You could also create a cheat-sheet which you print out and hold near you on your coaching calls with 10 or 15 examples of questions to ask. Choose questions that feel comfortable for you, and over time as you use them and find that some get the best responses and results in your coaching practice, add to them, subtract from them, and edit them so that they become uniquely yours.

Your questions should be crafted in such a way that they lead your client to not only choose to change, but also to become emotionally compelled to change, so that the change will be driven internally, rather than being imposed from the outside. This will lead to the highest level of change and accomplishment in your client, which will give you and your client the highest level of results and satisfaction.

Key Points

- Use questions to help clients take ownership of their challenges and the process necessary to achieve change.
- Pattern of questioning: identify the challenge, ask how the challenge is holding someone back, ask about the impact of that challenge, ask what it would mean to overcome the challenge, and ask how it would feel to overcome the challenge.
- When you lead your client to become emotionally involved in the change-making process, you stimulate the highest level of long-term change and results.

Recommended Reading:

Coaching Questions: A Coach's Guide to Powerful Asking Skills by Tony Stoltzfus

Get more at AnyoneCanCoach.net

Chapter 5

Price

The price of your coaching should be based on the results your clients can achieve, the level of access they receive, the amount of specialization and exclusivity you choose to incorporate, and your own pricing preference.

How you price your coaching should be based on the results your clients can get; what it means for them to achieve those results; the level of access, specialization, and exclusivity you provide; and your own pricing preference. Let's start with assessing the results someone gets from working with you:

1. What exactly can you help someone with?
2. What kind of results can you assist someone in achieving?

Here are some examples. Let's say you're a health coach and your client is 30 pounds overweight, has limited energy, and gets out of breath while playing with his grandchildren. After working with you, your client might:

- Lose 10 pounds of fat
- Gain 5 pounds of muscle
- Have more energy
- Get more sleep (or less)

Because your client has lost weight and gained muscle, he feels better about himself, and he can do everyday tasks easier. Because he has more energy, he can accomplish more at work and perhaps even be considered for a raise or promotion, and he won't get out of breath playing with his grandchildren.

Perhaps you're a life coach and your client is depressed, fights frequently with his spouse, and hates going to work. After working with you, your client might:

- Have more self-esteem
- Have a better relationship with his spouse
- Have a better attitude at work
- Have a happier outlook

Higher self-esteem and a happier outlook on life are benefits themselves. Because your client has a new attitude at work, he might be considered for a raise or promotion. If he isn't fighting with his spouse as much, your coaching may save his relationship or help him look forward to coming home at the end of the day.

Or perhaps you're a business coach and your client has revenues of $250k per year, costs of $125k per year, and works 60 hours per week. Your coaching might help him:

- Increase revenue by 10%
- Decrease expenses by 10%
- Reduce his work time by 2 hours per day
- Increase his job satisfaction

Because revenue is up 10% ($25k) and costs are down 10% ($12.5k), net profit is up $37.5k. Because your client is achieving all of this in 8 hours a day instead of 10–12, he has more time for his spouse, his family, and his hobbies.

In each of these scenarios, what is it worth to your client to achieve those results? In the health scenario, it might be worth $3,000 or less. In the life coaching scenario, it might be worth $2,000–$5,000 or more to your client. And in the business scenario, those results might be worth . . . $7,500 or more. Each individual client will have a unique value that he places on your coaching. For example, one client might be willing to pay more than another to lose weight and have more energy, one client might be willing to pay more than another to become more efficient at work and improve family relationships, and another client might be willing to pay more than someone else to increase revenue and improve his lifestyle.

How you price your coaching is also affected by the level of access you include. If you include a higher level of access, such as additional email, instant messenger, telephone, live event, or one-on-one access, you can charge more than for streamlined coaching that contains less access.

What you choose to charge is also influenced by the level of specialization in your coaching program. For example, imagine you are a health coach. You might specialize by coaching people who want to change their health radically, live longer, and get more out of life; or you could specialize by coaching people who have a specific health need; for example, weight loss, chronic fatigue, or sleeplessness. You could tailor your coaching to individuals with similar psychographic profiles; for example, people who are crunched for time, people who work at home, or people who work in unhealthy environments. You could tailor your coaching to individuals who are in a particular field or have attained some level of occupational or financial success, or both; for example, you could offer health coaching for pilots, life coaching for surgeons, or business coaching for CEOs.

And finally, what you charge is affected by your personal pricing preference. When you charge less, more people will enroll, but the time you spend with each client will be reduced. When you charge more, you will work with fewer clients, but you will be able to spend more time with each client.

So it really comes down to a choice for you. Do you want to work with more people in a less individualized way and charge less? Do you want to work with fewer people, in a more individualized and specialized way, and charge more? Or do you want to work with both segments of the market, creating two coaching programs, one offered at a lower price to appeal to a broader market, and another offered at a higher price to a more segmented portion of your market?

STRUCTURE YOUR PRICING

Once you have determined the value of your coaching, you can determine how to structure the price. For example, do you want to charge a one-time fee for working with you, or do you want to offer monthly payments? Or both? Once again, as with determining the core value of your coaching so that you can price it, the optimal pricing structure for your coaching is impacted by multiple variables such as psychographics, depth of the coaching, coaching access, your personal pricing preference, etc.

Here are some possibilities or examples of coaching pricing structures:

12-month coaching program with a high level of access: $5,000, or 12 monthly payments of $425.

6-month coaching program with a medium level of access: $2,000, or 6 monthly payments of $350.

Monthly coaching program with a high level of access: $500 per month, or prepay $5,000 for one year.

Let's assume you have 3 coaching program levels: introductory, intermediate, and advanced. You might have pricing that looks like this:

Introductory-level coaching program: 12 weeks for $500, or payments of $175 per month for 3 months.

Intermediate-level coaching program: 6 months for $1,500, or payments of $250 per month for 6 months.

Advanced-level coaching program: 12 months for $5,000, or payments of $425 per month for 12 months.

COMPETITORS' PRICING

The question often comes up, "What about competing on price with competitors who charge less?"

Your competitors' pricing structures can influence you when you get started, but I don't believe they should guide you long run. I believe most quality coaching is underpriced, so likely if you use your competitors' prices as your benchmark, you will also be underpriced; and if you don't price according to the factors we discussed earlier, for example, results, depth of training, etc., you will likely find you aren't charging enough to give enough of your time or your effort to help clients get the results they expect.

I believe that one of the biggest mistakes coaches make with their prices is to price so low that they are unable to deliver the quality of coaching that they have promised. Let's face it, if you underprice and oversell your coaching, you won't have the time or the energy to best help your clients. I believe it is better to have fewer clients at a higher price, and have them get better results because you can give them the attention for which they have paid, than to have many clients to whom you are unable to give appropriate attention.

So, what about your competitors' pricing structures? Here's my opinion: if you develop your coaching program the way I teach in this book, and focus on helping others rather than just making money, you will likely find that your coaching has an exceptional level of quality and delivers better results than your competitors' coaching programs—even if the elements in the programs appear to be the same (for example, the number of times you meet the client, the number of lessons, etc.). Because of this, it would be fine to price your coaching at a higher level than your competition. Will you lose some clients to your competitors' lower prices? Probably. However, will some clients enroll in your coaching after finding out that the lower-priced coaching of your competitors won't get them the results they want? Probably. And will some clients be willing to pay your higher price once they see that they can get better results as a result of working with you? Yes. By offering a higher level of potential results, giving better instruction, and working with your clients in such a way that they are getting a more complete experience than if they were working with your competition, you can easily charge more than your competition charges; in fact, you can set your own price, one that is not influenced by your competition's pricing structures, but is instead based on what it is worth to clients to interact with you.

When you first start out, it is okay to underprice your coaching to compete and feel good about the value you are delivering. But when you realize you are working with too many clients with too much access to deliver the best results, and you are getting positive feedback from successful clients that shows you that your coaching has a higher intrinsic value than that of your competition, don't be afraid to start raising prices. Over time, you will develop a feel for what your coaching is worth to your clients based on the time and quality you have put into your program, and rather than charging based on your competitors' prices, you can charge a fair price that reflects the level of results a client can achieve in working with you.

Key Points

- Price based on the results your clients can get, what it means for them to achieve those results, your clients' level of access to you, the level of specialization and exclusivity you build into your program, and your own pricing preference.
- Different segments of your market will pay more than others for your coaching.
- Generally speaking, the more you charge, the fewer people will enroll and the higher the overall quality you can deliver, and vice versa.

Recommended Reading:

Value-Based Fees: How to Charge - and Get - What You're Worth by Alan Weiss

Get more at AnyoneCanCoach.net

Chapter 6

When Clients Are Not Happy

No matter how good you are as a coach, you will experience an unhappy client from time to time. In most cases, you can make adjustments so that the client is satisfied and willing to continue to work towards results.

Your responsibility as a coach is to give your clients the tools and support necessary to get results. Each client's responsibility is to do the work necessary to get results. It is important to realize that not all clients will do the work. And this is where things get a little dicey for new coaches; they tend to have a difficult time separating their responsibilities from their clients' responsibilities. If some clients are getting results from following your training, that is usually a good indication that your training content is effective. You will also get positive (or negative) comments from clients about your teaching that will allow you to make changes to become more effective at helping people make change in their lives. However, each comment should not be taken just at face value, but instead you should ask yourself, "Is this comment realistic? Am I really doing that well in this area, or do I just connect very well with this client?" Or in the case of a negative comment, "Is that true, am I really doing poorly in that area, or is this an issue with this particular client?" It is easy to allow a few negative clients to lead you down a path of feeling that you are not effective, or that you are not connecting with your clients. Unfortunately, I can't give you a one-size-fits-all formula for how to tell the difference. You will simply need to use some intuition and thought to determine which it is in each scenario.

You will always have some clients who don't get results, because people only get results to the extent that they implement what you teach. And unfortunately many people won't implement what you teach. That doesn't make you a bad coach, and you should not allow it to detract from the results you can get with those clients who implement what you teach.

REFUNDS

Many times when a client signs up to work with you, he is excited about making real changes happen in his life, and he is likewise excited to work with you. However, after a few weeks or a few months of working with you, he realizes that he has to do some amount of work in order to achieve those changes, and for some reason he decides that he no longer wants to do the work. He might even want a refund for the coaching, since he isn't getting the results he thought he would get.

Assuming you are giving the right training for your client to get results (based on your experience, knowing that he is getting the right training to get results, if only he would implement what you teach; or based on the fact that other clients are getting results from implementing the same training), and knowing that it is your client's responsibility to do the work itself in order to get results, a refund is probably not the best option here. You see, coaching is a two-way street; both you and your client have a responsibility to do some work. And if your client isn't doing his work, I don't believe you should give that client a refund. And in fact, many times when you explain to the client that based on the time and commitment you have already put into the program, it simply isn't an option to give a refund, he will decide that since he has paid for the coaching anyway, he might as well continue. Explain to him that you realize that he hasn't gotten the results that he anticipated, and ask him why he thinks that is the case. Many people will tell you that they don't have as much time as they thought they would have, that they have become interested in something else, etc. At this point, you can ask him if he wants to make some adjustments to how you work together to get the best results out of the rest of the coaching for which he has already paid. Usually the client will be willing to do that, once he realizes that getting his money back is no longer an option.

Of course, you need to put a refund policy into place upfront in order to enforce it. Contrary to what you might hear from others, a money-back-if-you-don't-like-it policy is not necessary to get clients to enroll. You see, with coaching, it's not like just buying something that can be easily returned and resold. When you deliver coaching, you are sharing with someone your experience, which may have taken years to accumulate, and your time, which cannot be replaced. Meaning that if someone coaches with you, you can't simply replace the time you have already invested, so you can't just give his money back if he doesn't like it. I know this sounds harsh or unbending, but in reality, it is fair. And as you coach, you will see this to be the case. If you are a responsible coach, delivering what you promise, you will find that almost every instance where a client wants a refund is related to his not doing the work. And it's not your responsibility to reimburse your client for not holding up his part of the agreement.

Here is an example of talking with a client who is asking for a refund:

Client:

"I want a refund."

You:

"What's going on that has led you to want a refund; what's going on with the coaching?"

Notice I am reframing this request as an issue about the coaching itself (which it would be if the refund request should legitimately be considered).

Client:

"I want the refund because I'm not getting the results you promised."

You:

"OK, let's talk about it. Let's talk about the results you were hoping to get in working with me, and what's happened to hold those results back. Let's start with the results you were hoping to get; what exactly were you hoping to accomplish by this point in the coaching?"

Client:

(tells you what he hoped to accomplish)

You:

"What do you think is the biggest single factor why that hasn't happened yet?"

Client:

(tells you [this will rarely have anything to do with you; it will usually be something like time, not understanding the lessons, not doing the work, etc.])

Note: the rest of the discussion will be highly variable based on the response to the last question; on the following page there are a few examples:

You:

"So what do you think we can do to change that?"

Or:

"So it sounds like you haven't set aside the time we agreed upon; what do you think we can do to change that?"

Or:

"So it sounds like the lessons are moving a little too fast for you; we'll change that, add in more feedback, and get you back on track for achieving the results you want."

At this point, either the client agrees, or this may involve some more discussion. You may need to spend a little time going over the reasons why the client signed up in the first place (the results he wanted to achieve) and re-build the emotional desire for achieving those results. Most clients will agree to get back to doing the work so they can get back on track to getting the results they desire.

A client might tell you that he just doesn't want to do the work anymore, that he has changed his mind. At this point, it is time for you to simply enforce your policy. If your policy is that of no refunds on coaching, this conversation could go something like this:

You:

> *"I understand how you feel about this. However, it is your responsibility to do the work. I have put a lot of time and effort into not just creating your lessons, but also into the (time value, for example, 12 hours) we have spent coaching together. It's just not fair to me to refund you for all the time we have spent working together. I've put all of that time into this in good faith that you would do your part, but you haven't. So . . . a refund is out of the question.*
>
> *"However, I would be willing to make some changes to the coaching program by adding some more accountability into the program so that we work a little closer together to get these results, because that is my goal in working with you, to help you achieve those results. Does that make sense?"*

Nearly all clients will agree that that is fair, and accept that they can't get a refund on the time you've already put in. In the rare case that someone just doesn't want to go forward at this point, you could offer a refund on the unused portion of the coaching program, based on your hourly consulting rates. For example, if someone has signed up for a $2000 6-month training program, your hourly rate is $100 per hour, and you have invested 15 hours into working with your client, you could refund $500 of the original coaching payment. Notice I am not recommending refunding based on the time that has elapsed in the program itself (although you could do that if you wish). The reason is that when you sell a coaching program of a certain term length, for example, 6 months, the bulk of your time involvement is in the first portion of that term, because you are spending time creating the lessons, planning the work, and working with your client. Once you have delivered the lesson material and instructed your client, most of your time spent later in the term of the coaching program is spent on accountability and motivating your client to do the work you have already taught. Therefore, the bulk of your time and experience investment is in the early part of the coaching term, so if someone wants 50% back after 50% of the coaching term (for example, after 3 months in a 6-month program), but you have already invested what may be 90% of the total time and experience you will put in all together, it simply doesn't make sense to refund 50% of the coaching fee when only 10% of your coaching remains to be delivered. Perhaps it would make sense to refund the unused 10%, but not 50%.

If you are genuine about wanting to help people, refund requests will be few and far between. But when they occur, you should be prepared, and hopefully what I have just shared with you gives you some clarity on how to handle refunds.

Key Points

- The biggest reason for client unhappiness is lack of implementation and therefore lack of results. To work with an unhappy client, isolate the reason, then find a way to help the client get back on track.
- Although from time to time you may have clients who ask for refunds, rarely is a refund necessary. Most clients who ask for a refund are simply frustrated because of a lack of results; if you work with the client to create a new excitement for implementation, a refund is not necessary.

Get more at AnyoneCanCoach.net

Chapter 7

Determine The Words Prospects Use

The words prospects use to describe their challenges are the words that are most effective in communicating with and persuading those prospects.

In the chapters that follow, I'll be sharing with you my techniques for finding prospects; building relationships with those prospects using automated, personalized email communication; and selling your coaching to those prospects through sales letters, teleseminars, and free consultations. However, before I get into the details of marketing your coaching, I'd like to share with you some thoughts about choosing the language and words you will use in all your prospect communication. If you know the steps to marketing, relationship building, and selling, but don't have the words to use that connect with prospects, you won't develop the trust and relationship needed to enroll them in coaching and help them achieve their goals.

Sometimes there is a gap between what your prospect needs and what he is looking for. For example, let's imagine that you are a health coach, and you are talking with someone about improving his health. Your prospect might need to eat better, exercise more, and reduce stress in his life. But perhaps your prospect is thinking instead that he needs to lose weight, get stronger, and have more peace.

Although your coaching will meet his need, and give him the result he is looking for, the words he is using and thinking to describe his need are different than the words you might be using to describe your coaching. You are thinking along the lines of selling "eat better, exercise more, and reduce stress" coaching, but your prospect is thinking about enrolling in "lose weight, get stronger, and have more peace" coaching. Realistically, both of those sets of words include the same long-term meaning. But the second set uses the prospect's language. And in most cases, the prospect will take action on language that fits his own perception of his problem. So it is important to find out what the words are that prospects are using to describe their problems, and become comfortable using those words in describing your solutions.

Of course, I am only referring to rephrasing things when you can accurately do so. You cannot choose to use the prospect's language if her language is not an accurate reflection of what you can help her accomplish. For example, if someone's language is to "lose 40 pounds in a month" or "get rich overnight" and you know you can't provide that, you can't use that language. So you must use some judgement in choosing what words to use; they must not only be relevant to your prospects, but be accurate in meaning.

When you use someone's own internal language, the language she is most wired to respond to, you will get better results than using your own words.

Here's another example of how this works:

Let's imagine someone tells you she wants something that will: "*Teach me how to communicate more clearly with my husband.*"

If your response is along the lines of: "*Ok, I have a program that will teach you how to talk more clearly, listen more effectively, and get along with your family better,*" you elicit a different response from her than if you say, "*I have a program that will teach you specifically how to communicate more clearly with your husband.*"

Although both of those statements might accurately describe your program that teaches people how to communicate within the family (including with the husband), the second statement will resonate with your prospect because she is specifically using the words "*communicate with my husband.*" You are telling her exactly what she needs to hear, because those are the words she uses to think about what she needs. You are telling her in her own words that what you have is exactly what she needs.

Here is another example:

You:

"So what is your greatest challenge with (his problem)?"

Prospect:

"My greatest challenge is (x,y,z)."

You:

"So your greatest challenge is (x,y,z); how would it feel to overcome that challenge so you could have (a,b,c) ([a,b,c] is something he has already told you he wants, again, in his words)?"

You are cultivating a feeling of connection that amplifies and speeds up the process of building trust, simply as a result of using your client's language. You are increasing the odds that he will take action, simply by using his language.

Once you find out which words resonate and generate action with your prospects, and use those phrases repeatedly and consistently through your entire campaign, you increase the likelihood of your prospects connecting with you and taking action by enrolling in coaching.

HOW TO DISCOVER AND USE THE WORDS YOUR PROSPECTS USE

To find the words your prospects use to describe their challenges, ask your prospects what their challenges are and pay attention to the exact words they use. When you talk with prospects about their challenges in one-on-one conversations or in email exchanges, take note of the words they use to describe their challenges or problems, and record them in a word processing document. If you have a list of prospects, you can send an email that asks for their challenges. When your prospects respond, copy their responses into a word processing document.

Then, when you are going to write a new email for your email campaign, a new sales letter about your coaching program, or a new marketing piece, you can go to this word processing document to find phrases around which to write your copy. Your emails will likely have an increased level of receptiveness because you are using your prospects' words and thoughts in your communication with them—just as if you were talking personally and using their phrases in your conversation. Your sales letters and teleseminars will become stronger. Each bullet point in your sales letter or teleseminar can be derived from your prospects' language. Each paragraph, each story, and each section of your sales letter or teleseminar can use some of this language.

As you are using these phrases that are straight out of your prospects' minds in your squeeze page, your emails, your sales letters, and your teleseminars or webinars, you will find these phrases will help you create a continuity in your marketing campaign. This continuity will occur because each time your prospect reads a new email or a sales letter, he will be put back into the frame of mind that "it is like you are reading his mind" (which in some way you are).

This technique will allow you to connect deeply with your prospects, will lead to having more prospects hire you (become clients), and will result in greater rapport and increased trust among clients. This results in those clients investing more with you than if there were less rapport and trust.

When you use your prospects' words in your normal communication with them, you increase the level of bonding and trust that occurs and naturally builds over time. And by increasing that level of bonding, not only will you be able to do a better job enrolling clients, you will also be able to connect better with them so that you can help them achieve even greater results than if you were using language that doesn't resonate as well with them.

Key Points

- To connect best with your prospects and clients, find out the words they use to describe their challenges and problems.
- To find out what words prospects and clients use, ask questions through one-on-one conversations and emails.
- Use your prospects' language in emails, sales letters, teleseminars, and one-on-one conversations to deepen the trust and bond prospects have with you.
- When you use your prospects' language, not only do you enroll more clients, but those who do enroll get better results because they connect better with you.

Get more at AnyoneCanCoach.net

Chapter 8

Sell Using Free Consults

Free consults allow you to find out if or how you can help your prospects and enroll them in the best coaching program for their needs.

In the next few chapters, I'll be showing you a few ways to sell your coaching to prospective clients using free consultations (free consults), teleseminars, and sales letters. You can use these techniques alone or in combination, and over time, you will likely want to use all 3 methods, as each has a particular strength. Free consults yield the highest conversion rate (percentage of prospects who become coaching clients), but are the most time intensive. Teleseminars allow you to convert multiple clients simultaneously, but still require a time commitment from you; sales letters convert at the lowest conversion rate, but are highly efficient because once you write them, they convert prospects to subscribers consistently without any additional time or involvement from you. I'll start by teaching you how to do a free consult in this chapter, then I'll teach you how to deliver a teleseminar and write a sales letter in the next 2 chapters. Let's get started!

FREE CONSULTS

A free consult is a free one-on-one consultation during which you ask questions to find out if or how you can help a prospective client. If you are a good fit to work together, she may enroll and become a client. This free consult should be positioned as a high-value meeting that will:

1. Identify exactly what she wants to accomplish.
2. Determine what is holding her back from accomplishing that (identifying the root or source of her problems or challenges).
3. Suggest a solution to help her overcome her challenges and accomplish her goals.

The purpose of the call is to discover what your prospect really needs and guide her in making the right decision, whether that is enrolling in coaching with you, purchasing a training product, or something else. Some prospects may need something you don't provide. In that case, recommend the right person or solution for them. Other prospects may need something simple which doesn't require long-term coaching with you. This may be something you can simply teach on the free consult, or something you have taught in one of your information products. It may even be something you can teach in an hour or two of paid coaching. And of course, there will be prospects who need your coaching program, and during the free consults, you will show them that your program is the best solution to their problems.

A common mistake in selling coaching through free consults is in trying to "coach your heart out" to prove to your prospect that you will make a good coach. Unfortunately, that strategy usually backfires.

The reason is that if, during the free consult, you simply answer all of your prospect's questions and tell him what he needs to do to overcome his challenges (in short . . . coach him), at the end of the session he may be really appreciative to you for coaching or teaching him, but he will likely not follow through with the actions needed to overcome his challenges, just as he has not followed through in the past.

The fact is, he needs long-term coaching. His problem has developed over time. He has likely taken advice from others, read books, contemplated his problem, etc.; but he still has his problem or challenge. If you give him a band-aid solution on the free consult, he will likely not enroll in coaching; yet in a few months he will likely be in the same frustrating place as he was before he talked with you. He'll start looking for someone else to help him, and the negative cycle will continue.

Instead, ask questions to discover his challenges and problems during the free consult, and show him that your coaching solution will help him solve his problem long-term, once and for all. This is far more effective than telling him how to fix his problems on the spot, because that won't create long-term change.

With this method, your prospect gets more value from his session with you because he signs up for coaching. Even prospective clients who choose not to sign up with you receive more long-term value, because the questioning process stimulates thoughts that help them determine the true roots of their problems so that they can take the steps that are necessary to create change in their lives.

METHODS OF GETTING PROSPECTS ON THE PHONE FOR FREE CONSULTS

There are several effective ways to get prospects on the phone with you for free consults. The most popular methods are:

1. Sending out a personal email invitation
2. Sending out a mass email invitation
3. Offering an invitation on a teleseminar
4. Offering an invitation to buyers of an information product

All of these methods are effective, and are best used in combination over time. Some people may not respond to a mass email invitation, but may respond when invited personally. Some people may not respond to an email invitation, but may respond to a "free consult with purchase" offer, and so on; so over time, vary the methods you use to schedule free consults.

PERSONAL EMAIL INVITATION

This is one of my favorite methods of getting a potential client on the phone for a free consult. It works especially well for coaches who have a small pool of prospects, because it allows them to get the highest number of prospects on the phone from the smallest pool of prospects.

You simply ask someone through email, after having an email exchange discussing one or more of his challenges, if he'd like to get on the phone with you for a free consult. The initial email exchange begins one of two ways: either he writes you and asks you a question, or you send an email asking him if he has any challenges you can help him with. You can send the initial email through your autoresponder so it goes to multiple prospects, but once a prospect replies, all further communication is personal.

Your email to your prospects might look like the following example. I call this an "I need your help" email:

Subject line:

(Prospect Name)—I need your help

Body:

(Prospect Name),

I need your help. I am in the process of creating a brand new coaching program to help you with (something in your niche) and I want it to be exactly what you need to get you from where you are to where you want to be in 3–6 months.

So . . . I need your help.

1) *What is your goal for the next 3–6 months?*

2) *What are the 3 biggest things that are holding you back from accomplishing your goal?*

By the way, if you reply to this email with your answers within the next 48 hours, I promise to personally respond and try to help you achieve your goals.

Thanks in advance!

(Your Name)

Here's the psychology behind this email:

The subject line, "I need your help," generates interest. The email body tells your prospect why you need his participation. You are, in effect, seeding his mind with the idea that this program might be right for him, and if he participates by responding, it will be more highly customized for him and his needs. When he responds to this email, he is being psychologically primed to consider joining the program.

By asking for his time-oriented goals, you are leading him to visualize where he wants to be in a given time period. When he writes those goals down in his email response to you, he is creating a powerful affirmation of his desire to achieve his goals.

By asking him about what is holding him back from achieving his goals, you are leading him to think about not only what is holding him back, but also about the fact that without overcoming those challenges, he isn't going to achieve his goals.

Why three challenges? If you use just one challenge, his response tends to be shallower and reveal less information about what is really the problem. By asking for three, you'll get deeper, more thoughtful information from him. Three challenges also gives you the opportunity to help him for free with one challenge, but leaves two for paid coaching.

The reason to give a deadline is that it compels your prospect to respond faster. Time is of the essence here; because he is struggling with his problem now, the sooner you are able to present a solution, the better the chance he will enroll with you.

If someone doesn't answer both questions, he is likely not a strong prospect for your coaching. To someone who answers both questions completely, reply to his email and try to solve one challenge with a few sentences or less. If that's not possible, and you have written a tutorial, recorded a video, or recorded an audio teaching the answer, give him a link to access it. You are activating the law of reciprocity here, while revealing your expertise. For each of the remaining two challenges, ask at least one question (and no more than two or three questions per challenge) that allows you to dig deeper into the challenge.

For example:

"Tell me more about (the challenge)."

"What do you mean by (the challenge)?"

"How is that affecting you?"

"Why is that holding you back?"

Don't ask the same question for both challenges! This is a formula for you, but for your prospect, this should appear to be very genuine and natural. (And of course it should be genuine; you really want to see how you can help this person.)

Some people will not respond when you send this email. Don't try to chase these prospects; assume they are not ready for coaching from you yet. You will find that some people hang around asking questions for months before they finally choose to take real action with you.

How your prospect answers is generally indicative of his interest in getting help. If he answers hastily with one or two words, ask a few more questions, trying to get him to go deeper. If he won't, he probably isn't a strong prospect. The strongest prospects generally write much more. I believe this is a reflection of two things: 1) their trust level is higher, so they write more and 2) they are seriously interested in solving their challenges, thus they are willing to spend more time and write more. If you believe the prospect might be a good fit for your coaching, respond like this:

> *(Prospect Name),*
>
> *I can help you with this, but it is going to take more than a few emails back and forth. I suggest we get on the phone; we'll need about an hour, and I'll answer all your questions, show you exactly what to do to get to your goal, and give you a blueprint for achieving that. I'll also tell you about my coaching and ask you some questions to determine if you and I are a good fit to work together, as I don't work with just anyone. So let me know 3 times over the course of the next 7–10 days that are good for you, and I'll schedule it based on my availability.*
>
> *(Your Name)*

A number of people will not respond at this point. They may have decided they are not interested in coaching. Those who respond are generally qualified prospects. Set the earliest appointment you can based on the times your prospect gives you.

MASS EMAIL INVITATION

Another way to find prospects for your free consult is to send an email invitation to multiple prospects simultaneously using your autoresponder. It could look something like this:

Subject line:

(Prospect Name)—free consult with (Your Name) if you qualify

Body:

I have discovered that my schedule for next week contains a few hours of downtime, when I am not working with clients or have scheduled product production in place, so I have decided to reserve a few of those hours to give a few select clients a no-obligation, no-strings-attached one-hour consultation with me.

If you qualify for this free consultation, we will:

1) *Determine exactly what you want to accomplish in (something in your niche) in the next (time frame, e.g., 3–6 months).*

2) *Examine what is holding you back from accomplishing that goal and find out what possible roadblocks are stopping you.*

3) *Create a complete blueprint for exactly what you need to do to accomplish your goal.*

I only have a few spots available, and only want to help people who are already taking action to achieve their goals, so I have a few questions I need you to answer completely and honestly to determine if you are a good fit to talk with me:

1) *What is your goal for the next 3–6 months?*

2) *What are your 3 biggest challenges in achieving that goal?*

3) *What have you already tried to achieve your goal?*

4) *On a scale of 1-10, with 10 being the strongest, how important is it to you to achieve your goal?*

Just hit reply to answer these questions; I look forward to talking with you if you qualify.

To your success,

(Your Name)

Once someone has answered the questions and appears to be qualified, reply with an email like this:

Subject line:

(Prospect Name)—your requested free consult

Body:

(Prospect Name),

Right now my first available time for your free consult is (time and date). Will that time work for you?

(Your Name)

Once you have agreed on a time, write this email:

Subject line:

Re: (Prospect Name)—your requested free consult

Body:

(Prospect Name),

I have you confirmed for (time and date). What is your phone number?

(Your Name)

If the email is within several days of the appointment you do not need to confirm the appointment. If it is more than a few days before, send a confirmation email the day before the scheduled session to remind your prospect of the appointment.

TELESEMINAR INVITATION

You can also hold a teleseminar for the purpose of getting prospects to sign up for free consults. Use the same procedure for delivering the teleseminar as I teach in Chapter 9, but instead of selling coaching, give the opportunity to sign up for a free consult. This could sound something like this:

"This concludes the content I planned to cover today, and I can tell you this, although I really went deep into this topic, and gave you some great information you

can start implementing today to begin producing results, it is literally only the tip of the iceberg in terms of what I can ultimately help you with.

"For some of you, what I have taught today is all you need, and that's fine. In fact, that's great because you can take what I have taught today and begin implementing it now.

"But if you are thinking, 'I want to learn more; I want more than just the tip of the iceberg,' then I have a very special offer for you today. It's not a package of CDs or mp3s you have to buy today to learn more. In fact, it's not going to cost you anything but your time.

"Here's the deal . . . I have set aside 5 hours of time to give 5 people a full one-hour free consultation—literally no strings attached—and during that free consultation we will:

"Determine exactly what you want to accomplish in (something in your niche) in the next (time frame, e.g., 3–6 months).

"Examine what is holding you back from accomplishing that goal and find out what possible roadblocks are stopping you.

"Create a complete blueprint for exactly what you need to do to accomplish your goal in (time frame).

"Let's face it, not everybody needs this. So if you don't, that's OK. But if you want to spend an hour with me—and you can ask any questions you want—I will answer your questions and help you get on track and give you a blueprint for what to do to accomplish your goals.

"There are only 5 spots available. Since there are a lot more people than that on this teleseminar, I have a screening process that includes a short application with a few questions to help me determine who needs my help most. This is what I do best—help people achieve success fast—and to use my time most effectively, I want to work with the people who need my help the most.

"When I give you the link to the application, I suggest you go to it immediately and answer the questions, because I am going to look at the applications on a first-come, first-served basis, and once the slots are all taken . . . that's it. Here's the link: (link to the application)."

The application will ask for basic information, such as name, email, and telephone number, and ask these types of questions:

1. What is your goal for the next 3–6 months?
2. What are your 3 biggest challenges in achieving that goal?
3. What have you already done to try to achieve your goal?
4. On a scale of 1–10, with 10 being the strongest, how important is it to you to achieve your goal?

You can use your autoresponder service to create the survey, or a survey service like surveymonkey.com. (I have posted specific technical directions for creating the survey at AnyoneCanCoach.net.)

At this point on the teleseminar, you can teach a little more if you want, take a few live questions, or talk a little more about the advantages of filling out the application and talking with you, and give the link again. Don't try to sell anything. The purpose of this teleseminar is to get qualified prospects on the phone with you so you can determine if or how you can help them. After the teleseminar, schedule the free consults using the scheduling steps on pages 129-130.

FREE CONSULT WITH PURCHASE OF INFORMATION PRODUCT

You can include a free consult as a bonus when someone buys an information product. On your download page, or in a post-sale email to your information product buyer, invite her to schedule the session with you by sending you an email or by filling out a web form you have created using your autoresponder. Schedule the free consult using the scheduling steps on pages 129-130.

DELIVER THE FREE CONSULT

To deliver the free consult, use the telephone rather than another form of communication such as instant messaging or email, because the telephone itself serves as a qualifying mechanism. My experience has been that the majority of people who are unwilling to use a telephone call for a free consult are unlikely to be willing to pay for coaching. If your prospect asks to use instant messaging or email for the free consult, tell her you only use the telephone for this call. If she won't comply, assume she isn't qualified to work with you, and cancel the call.

I also suggest calling your prospect (as opposed to having him call you) so that you don't waste time waiting for him to call. People sometimes call too early, too late, or get time zones mixed up. Your time is valuable, so even waiting 5 minutes for someone to call in late is a waste of your time. The way to handle this is to make all the calls. If your prospect isn't ready when you call, that's fine; you can reschedule or call back in 5 minutes (knowing you have 5 minutes to work on something else without interruption). In either case, you remain in control of your time.

SAMPLE WORDS AND LANGUAGE FOR THE FREE CONSULT

In the process of showing you how to structure this call, I will be using sample words and language. However, the language itself isn't what enrolls clients; instead, it's the process, the questions, and the guided interaction with you that leads your prospects to become clients. Feel free to use any of my language in your own free consults, but you don't need to copy my language word for word. What's best is to internalize the process I use, then use words that are natural for you and that reveal who you are, not who I am.

The first step in the free consult is to remind your prospect what the call is about and to set the framework for the call. It's easier to follow your plan on the call when you've told your prospect what that plan will look like.

You can say something like this at the beginning of the call:

> *"(Prospect Name), let's go ahead and get started. The way this call is going to work is I am going to start by asking you some questions to determine if or how I can help you. I will be specifically looking at what it is you want to accomplish and what is holding you back from accomplishing it, and once we have determined that, I will recommend a solution for you. The only thing I ask is that at the end of the call, you tell me if that solution works for you or not. Is that fair?"*

There are a few specific things to notice here.

1. You are telling your prospect exactly what you will be doing on this call. This confirms what the call is about, and indicates that you will be offering a solution.
2. You are making it very clear that this call is about determining if or how you can help him, and then offering a solution. This relaxes the atmosphere of the call by taking away the pressure caused by fearing that your focus is to "sell" him.
3. You are getting his agreement that he will tell you if the solution works for him or not.

In the rare case that someone is not agreeable, is disrespectful, or seems determined to control the conversation, you can decide to end the call. If someone has an attitude or tone of voice you don't like, or if you're not interested in what she wants to work on, you can choose not to offer her coaching.

It's important to realize that this is your coaching business, and you can choose not to work with any prospect, just as she has the right to choose not to work with you. Tell the prospect that it sounds like she isn't a good fit to work with you. Most clients are easy to work with, so there's no point in taking on a client who will be difficult to work with.

Once you have established agreement about what you are going to do on the call, you can begin asking questions to determine if or how you can work together. Ask questions that will help you:

1. Find out where someone is at in his current journey (meaning what he has already accomplished or not accomplished towards his goal).
2. Find out what he wants to accomplish in the future.
3. Find out what is holding him back from accomplishing that goal.
4. Find out how it is having an impact on him to not accomplish that goal.
5. Find out what it will mean for him to accomplish the goal.

You can start with something like this:

"Let's start with your current situation, tell me exactly what is going on with your (whatever your niche is, for example, business, life, relationships, health, etc.)."

Once she starts telling you about her situation, listen actively. Ask relevant questions. If she tells you something general, and you need more details . . . ask.

As she tells you what is going on in her situation, she is usually telling you about the things that aren't working. You can ask a progression of questions like these about each problem or challenge:

"So tell me more about that . . . what's not working?"

"Why not?"

"How is that having an impact on your (business, health, life, etc.)?"

"How does that make you feel?"

"How much longer are you willing to continue struggling with that?"

"Are you ready to change that today?"

By asking these questions now, you are beginning to create agreement with the prospect that she would like to fix each problem. Then let her go back to telling you about the rest of her situation. Continue asking similar questions, digging to understand more about her problems, how bad they are, how they are having an impact on her, how much she wants to fix them, etc.

Once she has told you all about her situation and her problems with it, and you have asked her relevant questions based on what she has voluntarily revealed about her problems, you can say something like this:

> *"OK, (Prospect Name), I'd like to switch gears here for a few minutes . . . what exactly do you want your (business, life, relationship, etc.) to look like 3–6 months from now?"*

When she responds, you can ask a progression of questions like these:

> *"So how would it feel to accomplish that goal?"*

> *"What would it mean to you to accomplish that?"*

> *"What else would it mean to you?" (continuing to ask this question until you have exhausted what this accomplishment would mean to her)*

Then transition back to what she wants to accomplish:

"So, (Prospect Name), what else do you want to accomplish in the next 3–6 months?"

When she tells you, ask questions to zone in on what that specific accomplishment would mean to her. Continue this process, asking "*what else . . . ?*" until there is nothing else.

Allow her to paint as complete a picture as possible about what it would mean for her to accomplish her goal. You see, the bigger her dream, and the more effectively she can visualize how her life will be when she accomplishes the goals which you can help her accomplish, the easier it will be for her to make the decision to work with you. Next ask her what is holding her back from accomplishing her goal. You might say something like:

"Excellent, now the thing is, obviously you aren't going to be able to accomplish these things if you continue doing things the way you've been doing them, right?"

Of course she agrees. You continue:

"So let me ask you this, what is holding you back from accomplishing (name what she is trying to accomplish)?"

If you have already discovered what is holding her back from the things she is trying to accomplish, you might ask:

"So, we've talked about how (challenge one) and (challenge two) and (challenge three) are holding you back from being able to accomplish (name what she is trying to accomplish) and feel (the way she said she would feel if she could accomplish it).

"So let me ask you this, what else is holding you back from accomplishing (what she wants to accomplish)?"

When she tells you, you can use a progression of questions like these:

"How is that holding you back?"

"How is that having an impact on your (business, health, life, etc.)?"

"How does that make you feel, knowing that (name what is holding her back) is having an impact on your (business, health, life, etc.), and (name specifically how it is having an impact), and how that is holding you back from (what she is trying to accomplish)?"

"How much longer are you willing to continue struggling with that?"

"Are you ready to change that today?"

Then ask again:

"What else is holding you back from accomplishing (what she is trying to accomplish)?"

Continue asking the above question and discussing each response until she tells you there is nothing else that is holding her back.

In some cases, you will have someone tell you that there are only one or two things holding her back. In most cases when this occurs, she simply doesn't know or can't think of what is holding her back. If you have done a good job listening to what is going on in her situation, and you know what the common challenges are for her situation, you can ask some questions about things that have historically held back other prospects or clients in a similar situation. For example:

"So what about (something that could be holding her back), do you struggle with that?"

If she says, *"Yes,"* you can go to the usual progression of questions:

"How is that holding you back?"

"How is that having an impact on your (business, health, life, etc.)?"

"How does that make you feel?"

"How much longer are you willing to continue struggling with that?"

"Are you ready to change that today?"

Follow this up with:

"Is there anything else that's holding you back?"

Once you feel you have completely explored what the prospect wants to accomplish or achieve, what is holding her back from achieving it, and what it would mean to her for her to achieve it; determine the best solution for her, based on the questions you have asked and the answers she has given you.

The solution may not be your coaching program. It might be any one of the following possible solutions, a combination of these solutions, or something else entirely:

1. She needs something you can't provide.
2. She only needs some advice that can be given on the free consult itself.
3. She needs some information product or training you have created.
4. She needs some amount of one-on-one specialized coaching from you.
5. She needs to enroll in your coaching program.

If she needs something you can't provide, recommend, or give her direction on finding, someone who can provide what she needs. If she needs some advice that can be given on the free consult itself, give it.

If she needs training or coaching from you, tell her that you have a solution, training program, coaching program, etc. that can help her; and ask her if she would like you to tell her about it. This could sound something like this:

> *"(Prospect Name), I can help you overcome (the problem or problems you have been discussing) and achieve (the result or results she wants to achieve). Would you like me to tell you about my (name solution: coaching, training, coaching program, etc.)?"*

Or:

"(Prospect Name), I have a coaching program that will help you achieve (name things your program will help her achieve that are relevant to her needs). Would you like me to tell you about it?"

Once she responds affirmatively, get her agreement that if your solution is a good fit for her and she can afford it, she will purchase or enroll on the day of the call. It is important that you get her commitment to get started on the day of the call, before you get into the details of the program and the price.

Once you mention the price, it can cloud your prospect's judgment as to whether she should make this change in her life. However, whether or not she needs your solution has nothing to do with price. She either needs it or she doesn't.

If she has committed to working with you before you talk about price, then you know that the only thing you need to resolve is the price. That way you aren't trying to juggle two things: "does she want to do this?" and "is the price right?"

To do this, you can ask something like this:

"(Prospect Name), if I can show you that in the course of working with me (or participating in my coaching program, etc.) you will be able to solve (name the

challenge or challenges based on what you have discussed) and achieve (the results you have discussed that she desires), and it is affordable to you, are you ready to get started today?"

If she tells you she isn't ready to get started today, initiate a discussion about when she will be ready to get started. How long does she want to wait to get results? How much longer is she willing to continue to do things the way she has been doing them, before making a change in her life? What is holding her back from getting started today? You will either be able to show her successfully that she is better off starting now; or you will realize that no matter the price of your program, or anything else involved, she simply isn't ready.

If she isn't ready, give her an alternate step she can take. For example, perhaps there are some changes she needs to make, or actions she needs to take, before she will be willing to enroll in coaching with you. If that is the case, leave her with instructions for making those changes, and offer to get back on the phone when she is ready. But until she is ready to take action and get started, don't talk about the details of your coaching program and your pricing. This may seem counterintuitive, but if she has told you she is not going to get started with you, no matter what the program or the price is, there is no benefit to sharing that information now.

Once she tells you that she is ready to get started today if it is affordable to her, tell her about your coaching program.

DESCRIBE YOUR COACHING PROGRAM

When you describe your coaching program, focus on the results your prospect will get in working with you. Take time to describe each component of your program, why each component is critical to his success, and exactly what results he can expect to achieve as a result of each component. For example, if you have a 12-week training core, you might say:

> *"You are going to receive 12 training lessons that are going to teach you (exactly what you are going to teach) and when you have completed these lessons, this is what you will have in place in your (life, business, health, etc.)."*

Go into detail on the results he can attain as a result of doing the work in the program. To describe the interactional element, you might say something like this:

> *"You are going to receive 12 months of unlimited email access to me, as well as a total of 24 hours of small-group coaching. With the unlimited email access, you can get any question answered any time I am online (which is 9–5 Monday through Thursday, for example), so that you don't have to wait until the next group coaching call or lesson to continue in your coaching and work with me.*

"And with the small-group coaching, you are going to get 24 hours of access to me over the course of the year, in a small group of 5–10 others who have very similar challenges to yours. The advantage to that is that there is a real camaraderie that occurs on these calls. For example, many times someone on the call will ask something, and when I answer it, a lightbulb will turn on in your mind, and you will realize you can use whatever it is that I just shared with the other person, perhaps something you never would have thought to ask about. And of course you can build relationships with others in the group who have similar problems to the ones you have.

"Would that be valuable to you, interacting with other people who are learning the same thing at the same time as you?"

To describe the homework, you might say:

"You are also going to receive 2 homework assignments per month. These homework assignments will take about 5–10 hours each to complete, and as you complete each one, you will be implementing the exact steps necessary to achieve your goals. You see, I have found that if my clients just learn the material, but don't implement it, they don't get the same results as if

they had implemented the material, so I have added this homework component. The only thing is, you have to be willing to do the homework and get it back to me so that I can evaluate it and help you stay on track. Are you willing to do that?"

Once you have explained to your prospect everything he is going to receive, you can then tell him the price. Once you tell him the price, he will either choose to sign up, choose not to sign up, ask additional questions, or tell you he can't afford it. If he chooses to sign up, sign him up. If he chooses not to sign up, you can ask questions to determine if there are adjustments you can make to the program to make it a better fit for him, and answer any questions he might have about the program.

If he says he can't afford it, you can say:

"(Prospect Name), let me ask you this, if money weren't an issue at all, do you like the program? What do you like best about the program?"

Let him tell you what he likes about the program. Then you can say something like this:

"Here's why I'm asking . . . the thing is, I can't just discount this package just like it is, it wouldn't be fair to everyone who paid full price for it, right? But . . . if

we could adjust the program a little so you could afford it, and you get to keep everything you really love about the program . . . and if we could make a payment plan you could really afford, do you want to get started today?"

If he says, "*Yes,*" you can say:

"Ok, so how much can you afford to put down today?"

He might say, "*$1,000.*" You can say:

"Excellent, so we'll do $1,000 down today, and how much can you afford to pay each month?"

He might say, "*$500 per month.*" You can say:

"Excellent, so let's do this (amend the program a little, get his agreement that he likes the program) and what I'll do for you is $1,000 down today then $500 per month. I will go ahead and put together a coaching agreement that summarizes everything we have discussed, and includes a payment link to get started. Do you have any other questions about the program?"

Once someone has agreed to sign up for your coaching, you can say:

> *"Excellent, give me about 10 minutes to get this out to you; as soon as I get your payment I'm going to send out your first lesson; I want you to get started today, because tomorrow there are a couple of things that I'd like you to do so that you are ready for your first coaching call with me on (day of the week) . . . "*

(You can alternatively ask for his credit card info and take it over the phone, and send the agreement after taking payment. However, I prefer to send a payment link with the agreement, instead of taking the payment over the phone, because it results in stronger sales on average, and fewer cases of buyer's remorse.)

As in the above example, give your prospect at least one reason to get started and make the payment today. If he doesn't sign up today while his excitement is high, he may talk himself out of enrolling. However, since he needs your program, if he talks himself out of it, he won't be able to achieve the things he told you he wants to achieve. And of course, if he doesn't sign up, you won't have a new client.

SAMPLE FREE CONSULT

Following is a transcript of a hypothetical (yet realistic) free consult so that you can see how easily these parts fit together; you can also use it as a study guide to become comfortable with the process.

You:

"Hello, is this (Prospect Name)?"

Prospect:

"Yes, it is."

You:

"Hi, this is (Your Name), is this still a good time for your free consult?"

Prospect:

"Yes."

You:

"(Prospect Name), let's go ahead and get started. The way this call is going to work is I am going to start by asking you some questions to determine if or how I can help you. I will be specifically looking at what it is you want to accomplish, and what is holding you back from accomplishing it, and once we have determined that, I will recommend a solution for you. The only thing I ask is that at the end of the call, you will tell me if that solution works for you or not. Is that fair?"

Prospect:

"Yes, that's fair."

You:

"Let's start with your current situation, tell me exactly what is going on with your (whatever your niche is, for example, business, life, relationships, health, etc.)."

Prospect:

"Well what's going on is that I don't have the focus I used to have, I'm not getting along well with my wife, I'm not as productive at work as I used to be, and I just don't have the energy I used to have. That's why I scheduled this session, because I am thinking that maybe all of this is tied together, that maybe my priorities aren't in the right place, and I'm not taking care of myself the way I should be."

You:

"So tell me more about the lack of focus . . . what's going on there?"

Prospect:

"I just can't seem to focus on anything for more than 5–10 minutes at a time."

You:

"How is that impacting you in your day-to-day life?"

Prospect:

"It is making it hard for me to get things done at work, or even around the house."

You:

"How does that make you feel, knowing that you really should be able to focus longer than that?"

Prospect:

"Well, obviously I don't like it, I mean, that's why I'm on this call with you."

You:

"So it sounds like you really want to change this . . . so let me ask you this, what exactly is going on with your wife, not getting along as well lately?"

Prospect:

"Well, really I think it is related. It's like I really want to focus and give her the attention she needs, but I get so easily distracted, and that really bothers me."

You:

"So, what do you think it is, I mean, what is making it so hard for you to focus and pay attention?"

Prospect:

"That's just it . . . I can't really put a finger on it, but it's really making me feel like I am losing out on all life has to offer right now."

You:

"You are right—you are definitely losing out by not being able to focus. And that's why we're on this call today, to get to the bottom of it, and come up with a solution. That's what you are looking for in talking with me, right?"

Prospect:

(laughing) "Yes, of course, I want you to fix it for me!"

You:

"I might not be able to just snap my fingers and fix it for you, but I will be able to assist you in fixing it yourself, and later on in this call, I'll share with you exactly how I do that. In the meantime, let's talk about what's going on at work, with your low productivity."

Prospect:

"Well it's almost like I feel the same way at work as I do in my relationship with my wife right now, that I can't focus so I'm not getting things done. It's really putting me in a bad position, because I am due for a promotion, but that isn't going to happen if I don't start focusing."

You:

"Yes, that's right. And my guess is that is tying in to your low energy as well, you aren't focusing so your energy is low, is that right?"

Prospect:

"Yes, you've hit the nail on the head there, and I feel like if I can just get my focus back, everything else will fall into place."

You:

"So it seems pretty clear that the #1 thing we need to work on in the coaching is getting your focus back, and perhaps do some work to help with your energy level,

in addition to working on some techniques to make it a little easier to pay attention both at work and with your wife, while we are getting your focus in place. So let me ask you this, if we could zoom forward 90 days, what do you want your life to look like 90 days from now?"

Prospect:

"It would be wonderful just to have my focus back. I would be getting along better with my wife, things would be going a lot better at work, I'd probably have the promotion I mentioned, and I would have a lot more energy and feel a lot better about work."

You:

"How would that feel, to be getting along better with your wife, get that promotion, and have more energy?"

Prospect:

"Wow! That would really feel great, like I have my old life back!" (laughing) "I'm glad I decided to get on this call with you!"

You:

"Great, well obviously if you keep doing what you are doing, you aren't going to get the change you want, so we will have to make some changes in your day to day life to help you get that focus back. So let me ask you this, what do you think is the single biggest thing that is holding you back from having that focus in place like you used to?"

Prospect:

"I think the biggest thing is that I don't really have a big goal I am shooting for. In the past, I would focus on improvement at work, or my wife and I were focused on achieving some things together, but now that things are comfortable it is like there is nothing to really shoot for; I think that is the biggest thing."

You:

"So what else do you think is holding you back right now?"

Prospect:

"I think that another thing is that I don't have the same energy level I used to have. The funny thing is, before we talked, I was thinking that was a result of the focus issue, but maybe a little bit of it is the other way around. I'm not eating as well as I used to, and I've gained some weight, so I don't have as much energy, and maybe that's hurting my ability to focus."

You:

"Yes, that could definitely be an issue there, we can work on that together, to help you get your eating habits right and your energy level back. So . . . how would that feel, to have your energy level back to what it used to be?"

Prospect:

"Well, like I said, that would be great, it would really feel good."

You:

"Excellent—well in a few minutes I am going to offer you a program to work with me where you and I can work together to get that energy back, and get your focus back. Are you excited about that?"

Prospect:

(laughing) "You bet I am . . . I am really excited about working with you!"

You:

"Great, I look forward to helping you as well . . . so is there anything else you can think of that is holding you back right now, aside from your energy level, and the big lack of new goals to motivate you and lead to some real focus?"

Prospect:

"No, I think that's about all."

You:

"Great, well let's talk about how we can work together. I am going to recommend a very specific course of action for you that will get you back on track, get your energy level back, and get your focus back both at work and at home with your wife. It will require some work on your part, as well as on mine; are you willing to put a few hours a week into changing your life like this?"

Prospect:

"Yes, absolutely!"

You:

"Great! So let me ask you this before I share with you the details on how we will work together. If you can see that it will get you the results we've been talking about, and it fits within your budget, are you ready to get started today?"

Prospect:

"Yes."

You:

"Great; here's how it is going to work: You are going to receive 12 training lessons that are going to teach you exactly how to get that focus back and regain your lost energy. We are going to especially focus on making that happen at work and with your wife first, but as time goes on, you will find that you have more focus and energy in the rest of your life as well.

"You are also going to receive 12 months of unlimited email access to me, as well as a total of 24 hours of small-group coaching. With the unlimited email access, you can get any question answered any time I am online (which is 9–5 Monday through Thursday), so that you don't have to wait until the next group coaching call or lesson to continue in your coaching and work with me. And with the small-group coaching, you are going to get 24 hours of access to me over the course of the year, in a small group of 5–10

others who are also dealing with focus and energy issues. The advantage to that is that there is a real camaraderie that occurs on these calls. For example, many times someone on the call will ask something, and when I answer it, a lightbulb will turn on in your mind, and you will realize you can use whatever it is that I just shared with the other person, perhaps something you never would have thought to ask about. And of course you can build relationships with others in the group, who have similar problems to the ones you have. Would that be valuable to you, interacting with other people who are learning the same thing at the same time as you?"

Prospect:

"Yes, that would be great; sometimes I feel like if I just had someone to talk with about all of this, I would have more focus!"

You:

"Great, well you are also going to receive 2 homework assignments per month. These homework assignments will take about 5–10 hours each to complete, and when you complete each one, you will be implementing the exact steps necessary to get your focus back, improve your productivity at work, and improve your relationship with your wife. You see, I have found that if my clients just learn the material, but don't implement it quickly, they don't get the same results, so

I have added this homework component. The only thing is, you have to be willing to do the homework and get it back to me so that I can evaluate it and help you stay on track. Are you willing to do that?"

Prospect:

"Yes, of course, I really want to get this fixed as soon as possible!"

You:

"Great, do you have any more questions for me about the program?"

Prospect:

"It all sounds great, but I have to ask . . . how much is this going to cost?"

You:

"I'll get to that in just a moment, but let me ask you first . . . what do you like best about this program and about working with me?"

Prospect:

"I really like the fact that I can email you anytime I have a question, and I also like the homework. I find that if I have something tangible to work on, it really helps me maintain my focus level."

You:

"Yes, a lot of my other clients like those 2 components as well. Well it sounds like to me you are ready to get started in the program, are you ready to get started?"

Prospect:

"Yes, let's do it!"

You:

"Great, well like we said earlier—we just need to finalize the payment. It is hard to put a monetary value on the results you are going to receive, in being able to focus again, giving you the chance to get that promotion, and of course being able to get along better with your wife now as well. And the truth of the matter is, if money weren't an issue, it would be truly priceless to be able to communicate better with your wife, get promoted, have more energy, and have a lot more focus, right?"

Prospect:

"Yes, indeed!"

You:

"But the truth of the matter is, I will be putting a lot of my time into the program as well, in addition to the unlimited email access, and the 24 hours of small-group coaching you will be getting. Normally, if you were to purchase coaching with me on an hourly basis, you'd be looking at about $300 an hour, so there is literally about $10,000 in real-world value of my time going into this program and working with you to assist you in getting your life back in shape. However, because I believe you are going to get the best results in working in a small group with others who are going

through something similar, I am going to be able to discount it significantly today. And that is what you are looking for, right, a bit of a discount to get started?"

Prospect:

(laughing) "Yes, of course!"

You:

"Great, so like we said, the real-world value of the program is $10,000; however, today I am going to discount it for you to $4,000. You can either pay for it in full up front, and you get an additional $500 discount; or you can put $1,000 down, and make 6 monthly payments of $500; which works better for you?"

Prospect:

"Well, that was a little more than I was anticipating investing today, but I guess I really need this. So if I pay for it in full today, it is how much?"

You:

"You will get a $500 immediate discount, so that would make it $3,500 today."

Prospect:

"Ok, that sounds fair, how do I pay?"

You:

"I will go ahead and put together a coaching agreement that summarizes everything we have discussed, and includes a payment link to get started.

Is a credit card okay with you, or do you want to use your checking account?"

Prospect:

"A credit card will work for me."

You:

"Great, give me about 10 minutes to get the agreement and payment link out to you. As soon as I get your payment I'm going to send out your very first lesson; I want you to get started studying today, because tomorrow there are a couple of things that I'd like you to do so that you are ready for your first coaching call with me on Thursday."

Prospect:

"Great, I am really excited about this, and getting my focus back!"

You:

"I am too. I think you will progress quickly; the key is going to be following along with the lessons and doing the work I assign. Well, if you don't have any more questions, I'll go ahead and get this out to you so you can get started."

Prospect:

"Great, I look forward to it!"

As you can see, in this example there isn't a lot of push-back from this hypothetical prospect about needing my help. That is usually the case with people who enroll; they are on the call with you because they really want to change things in their lives. If someone is making it difficult for you to ask questions, and not cooperating, ask him if he really wants to make some changes in his life. One of two things normally occurs: either he will agree that he is not serious, and you end the call early; or he will generally backpedal, apologize, and quite likely sign up for coaching at the end of the call.

I purposely chose something general (focus) as the thing this prospect wanted to change, so it's really easy for you to substitute in whatever change your client wants. This free consult pattern works well in just about all cases where your coaching is designed to help someone make a change of some kind. It works well in the health niches, for example, weight loss, energy, eating better, etc.; the business niches, for example, improving revenue, improving any area of performance, streamlining business, learning new tactics, etc.; and the life coaching niches, for example, communication, relationships, work-life balance, time management, etc. In short, you can use this script in whatever niche you are in, because the focus isn't on the exact problem your prospect faces; instead, it's on what that problem means for him, how not changing is impacting him, and what changing his life with your help will mean for him.

REVIEW OF DISCOVERY CALL SELLING PROCESS

1. Set up the expectation. Tell your prospect you are going to be asking questions to find out if or how you can help him.
2. Ask questions to find out what you need to know to determine if you are a good fit to work together, and to lead your prospect into determining how he can best move forward to achieve his goals.
3. Suggest a solution to his challenges. Sign up qualified prospects.

If this is new for you, you must practice. Don't give up even if your first 5, 10, or 20 calls result in no-sales. Instead, study each call to determine what you could have done differently.

If you give up after 5, 10, or 20 calls, or even more, that would be like going to a karate class and giving up after you try a certain kick or punch 5, 10, or 20 times, or even more, and you just don't have it right. It might take months to conquer that particular kick or punch, but it would be well worth it.

The same is true about learning to sell coaching. It will take time to master it. But once you do, it will be worth it. It will be a skill no one can take away from you. You'll be glad you put the time and effort in to learn it!

Key Points

- Use free consults to find out if or how you can help your prospects and enroll them in coaching.
- Don't coach on the free consults; instead, use the time and process to uncover client needs and possibly recommend coaching.
- You can use personal invites, mass email invites, teleseminars, and "free consult with purchase" offers to invite prospects to free consults.

Recommended Reading:

How to Master the Art of Selling by Tom Hopkins (the classic selling and closing manual)

Close the Deal by Sam Deep-Lyle Sussman

The New Conceptual Selling by Robert B. Miller and Stephen E. Heiman with Tad Tuleja

Additional Training:

freeconsultsellingsystem.com
sellingcoaching.com

Get more at AnyoneCanCoach.net

Chapter 9

Sell Using Teleseminars

Teleseminars allow you to share the value of your coaching program with multiple prospects simultaneously.

A teleseminar is a conference call on which you can talk with multiple prospects simultaneously. Using teleseminars to sell coaching is highly efficient because it allows you to sell to multiple prospects simultaneously.

If you have nurtured the relationship with your list in such a way that your subscribers not only trust and respect you, but also believe that you can teach them what they need, and you give great content on the teleseminar, a percentage of those listeners will choose to enroll in coaching with you.

The first thing to do is to choose a teleseminar topic. This should be a topic that is taught in your coaching program, and preferably is something your subscribers have told you they want to learn. Once you have determined what you will teach, schedule the teleseminar using a teleseminar service. (I have listed a few at recommendedteleseminars.com.)

Next, create a new sub-list in your autoresponder service. You will want everyone who is going to attend the teleseminar to be added to a sub-list separate from your main email list, so that you can communicate directly with them after the teleseminar. Some people do not buy during the teleseminar, but instead they think about the offer and then make a decision. However, if you don't remind them of the offer after the call, and encourage them to ask questions, fewer people will enroll.

Once you have created the new sub-list in your autoresponder service, create a page on which the subscribers can sign up for the teleseminar. You can create one using your autoresponder or teleseminar service, or create a custom sign-up page on your website. After creating the sign-up page, send 2–3 email invitations to attend the teleseminar. Send the first email 3–10 days before the teleseminar, the second email a couple of days before the teleseminar, and the third email the day before the teleseminar.

Here are samples of emails to send:

Email #1 (3–10 days before the teleseminar):

Subject line:

(Recipient Name)—Do you want to learn about (x,y,z)?

Body:

(Recipient Name), do you want to learn about (x,y,z)?

If so, I am teaching a live teleclass on (day, date, and time; for example, Friday, December 14th at 2 PM EST) where I will be teaching you: (primary topic you will be teaching).

You will learn: (3 bullet points for specific takeaways of interest to your audience)

> *Bullet one*
> *Bullet two*
> *Bullet three*

To sign up and receive access information:
(link to sign-up page)

(Your Name)

Email #2 (1–3 days before the teleseminar):

Subject line:

(Recipient Name)—(some legitimate claim about what you are going to teach)

Body:

(Recipient Name),

(a one- or two-sentence statement about the legitimate claim about what you will teach)

I will show you how on day, date and time (for example, Friday, December 14th at 2 PM EST) where I will be teaching you:

(primary topic you will be teaching)

You will learn:

(3 bullet points for specific takeaways)

> *Bullet one*
> *Bullet two*
> *Bullet three*

To sign up and receive access information:
(link to sign-up page)

See you on (Day)!

(Your Name)

Email #3 (the day before the teleseminar):

Subject line:

Urgent—Live training tomorrow at 2 PM EST

Body:

(Recipient name),

At 2 PM EST tomorrow (day of week, e.g., Thursday) I am teaching: (primary topic you will be teaching).

You will learn:

(3 bullet points for specific takeaways)

> *Bullet one*
> *Bullet two*
> *Bullet three*

To sign up and receive access information:
(link to sign-up page)

See you on (Day)!

(Your Name)

These are sample emails. Obviously you will vary them from call to call. There is no specific formula you need to follow, although you might notice that among the samples there is one email with a subject line related to the topic of the call, another with a subject line that intends to inspire interest and curiosity, and a final one that denotes urgency. (It is urgent; if someone doesn't sign up now, she will miss the training.) When you send out the second and third emails, exclude from the mailing anyone who has already signed up for the call.

Send a series of reminder emails to the people who have signed up. Send a reminder email the day before the call, a reminder email the morning of the call, another reminder one hour before the call, and another one (indicating that the call is starting NOW) 10 minutes before the call.

You can also send text messages or voice mails before the call, and suggest registrants add the teleseminar time to their calendars or schedule. The more qualified prospects you get on the call, the more people will enroll in your coaching.

DELIVER THE TELESEMINAR

The primary purpose of the call is to sign up new clients. The secondary purposes are to educate your prospects, and create additional rapport and credibility. For the teleseminar to be a success, you must do these things effectively:

- You must deliver the promised content.
- You must show prospects that you could be the right coach for them (if you and they are a good fit to work together).
- You must give them an opportunity to sign up for your coaching.
- You must do all of this in a way that comes together naturally, so that this can all be accomplished smoothly during the time of the call.

If you spend all of your time teaching, and at the very end make a quick offer for coaching . . . the most responsive prospects might enroll, but your enrollment percentage will be low. But if you spend too much time selling your coaching, you will offend those who wanted to learn from you. They might have signed up for coaching, but because they feel you are "overselling," they won't sign up. Therefore you want to give a strong presentation of content, in addition to letting prospects know about your coaching program.

A few minutes before the call is scheduled to begin, get on the conference line, and welcome people as they are coming onto the call. Tell them when the call will start; small talk a little and ask people their names, where they are calling from, etc. If you have done a few calls in the past, or if you've been developing relationships through email, there will usually be people on the call with whom you have been chatting online and are thrilled to be live on the call with you, and will tell you so. Roll with it, because talking with them live builds rapport and creates a deeper bond.

Once the scheduled time occurs, mute the line so attendees can only hear you, and not each other. Begin by telling them what the call will be covering, repeating the bullet points from the email you sent to them, and reminding them why they are here and what they are going to learn on the call. You can also give a brief (less than 5 minutes) biography of yourself as it pertains to the topic you are teaching, although this is not necessary. Give a complete overview of everything you will be teaching. At this point you can tell them that you will be making an offer at the end of the call. This might sound something like this:

> *"Folks, over the course of the next 45 minutes or so, I am going to be teaching in depth on ______ and _______ and I will be teaching you how to _______ and how to _______ and ______. I am going to teach my heart out, and for those of you who have been following me for some time or are enrolled in one of my coaching programs, you know that I really deliver the content on a teaching like this. But let me tell you this: I have literally taught for dozens of hours on this topic, providing incredibly deep information, and as much as I try to overdeliver on this call, I just won't be able to teach dozens of hours of solid information in 45 minutes. It's just not physically possible.*

"So I have decided to pull together a lot of my teachings—dozens of hours of intense teachings on this topic—and if you like what I am getting ready to teach you, you will LOVE the program I have prepared for you. I'll tell you all about it once I finish teaching this valuable information . . . so let's get started, shall we?"

Then teach for about 45 minutes. At the end of each major point, you can say something like this:

"Was that good information? Do you think you can use this in your life? As I said earlier, this is only the tip of the iceberg; I literally have hours of teaching on this topic, really in-depth information. At the end of the call, I will show you how you can start learning even more from me today."

As you move towards the end of the teaching content, transition to telling them about your program and your offer.

THE PROGRAM YOU OFFER

The offer will vary depending on the audience of the call. For example, if the people on the teleseminar are prospects and have never purchased anything from you, this offer might be your entry-level coaching program or product. If you are doing the teleseminar with an audience of people who have already purchased your entry-level offer, then this will be a higher-value coaching program. You can also design a teleseminar-offer-only information package containing recorded teaching, some limited coaching access, and a step-by-step daily guide; it might look something like this:

- 20 hours of in-depth teaching on the topic ($1,000 value)
- A 30 day step-by-step daily instructional guide ($1,000 value)
- Email access to you for any questions ($1,000 value)
- Access to several recorded calls with prior clients (with the clients' permission, of course) ($500 value)

Plus bonuses:

- A complete program you normally sell for $1,000
- A second program you normally sell for $1,500

This gives you a package that has a real-world value of $6,000, but could be offered at a significant discount to teleseminar participants, perhaps at $1,000, creating an incredible value for those who take action on the call. This type of package is very easy to produce, and yet can be sold time and time again for $1,000 or more at a consistent 10% conversion rate on a well-executed teleseminar.

MAKING THE OFFER

Once you have completed the teaching, present the offer for the coaching program or information package. Tell your participants why you are making a special offer, what is in the package, the value of the package and of the results they can achieve by implementing what is in the package, and make it easy for them to take action and buy the package or program.

SAMPLE CLOSE

Here is a sample close you can use as a guide and adjust to your style and comfort level:

"So far I have given you (repeat back a quick review of everything you have taught on the call so far) and although this has been a lot of amazing information, it is only the tip of the iceberg in terms of what you can learn from me on this topic. So the question is . . . do you want to implement what I have taught you today?

"For some of you, what I have taught is all you need. In fact, you may have almost all of the missing pieces

now, and are able to finish what you are trying to accomplish with what I have just taught you.

"However, for most of you, you are likely thinking, 'Wow! If that is only 5% of what (Your Name) can help me implement right now, then I want the other 95%.'

"You see, there are 2 ways you can learn to do something. You can try to figure it out on your own, which takes time and trial and error, and is likely holding you back from the success you really want. What's more, you might still be missing some critical pieces.

"Or you can let someone teach you how to do it. By letting someone teach you, you can start having success now, rather than waiting until you finally figure it out on your own.

"So with your permission, I'd like to share what I have prepared for you; so that instead of muddling through things with trial and error, hoping against hope that you don't take another wrong turn, you can learn how to get on the right path fast, starting today.

"I have designed a master program that includes complete teaching on (the program topic)."

Next:

- Describe everything the program is going to teach.
- Explain the results someone will have achieved in your program once he has completed it.
- Explain anything else you are putting into the program.
- Describe the value of everything that is going into the program.
- Describe any bonuses you are adding for taking action today and signing up today, and the value of those bonuses.
- Give the price at which someone can sign up today, then give the url to the sign-up page.

This might sound something like this:

> *"I have recorded over 20 hours of in-depth teaching on (topic of the teaching), including:*
>
> *"(first thing the program teaches), (second thing the program teaches), (third thing the program teaches) . . . and so on . . .*
>
> *"This is total of 20 hours of in-depth teaching, and when I sell it separately, I sell it for $1,000 or more.*

"I'm also including a 30 day step-by-step daily instructional guide which is going to give you exact instructions each and every day for 30 days on exactly what to do and how to do it to accomplish (something someone will accomplish by studying and implementing the material in your course). I don't normally sell this separately, but if I did, it is worth over $1,000.

"You are also going to get 30 days of email access to me for any questions you might have about implementing my techniques, and this is normally only included in my $1,000 a month coaching program.

"Plus, you are going to get access to several recorded calls with clients where I have taught them personally how to (list some of the things you teach on these recorded calls) . . . and this is something that normally would sell for $500.

"So this is a total value of $3,500 right now, but just for people who sign up today from this special teleseminar, I am going to throw in my (name of program) that normally sells for $1,000, plus my advanced (name of program) that normally sells for $1,500, which brings the total value of this package to over $6,000.

"However, I want to make this a no-brainer for you today, so if you go to (url link to purchase page) now, I am going to slash $5,000 off the price, and you'll only pay $1,000, or you can make 4 easy payments of $250 each.

"To review, this is what you are going to get if you take action now: (name each component, what each component will teach, and the value of each component)

"To get immediate access to all of this training, go to (url to purchase training) now and get signed up right away.

"Folks, I look forward to working with you to (whatever your coaching is going to help them with)."

That concludes the teleseminar. This will not necessarily go as smoothly as you would like the first time you hold a selling teleseminar. However, the formula is simple:

- Tell at the beginning of the call that you will be teaching powerful concepts on the call.
- Teach everything you indicated in the pre-call announcements that you would teach.

- Make an irresistible offer to invest with you to learn everything you couldn't teach because you only had 45 minutes.
- Focus more on over-delivering the content than on selling the program.

Keep in mind, any of the "words" I have given you as samples are just that . . . sample words. You are more than welcome to use them exactly as I have scripted them, but I recommend changing them to fit your style, comfort level, and own speech patterns. Delivering a teleseminar and making sales from it should be something that is easy to do, and doesn't need to be highly scripted. And especially if you plan to do these regularly, as a combined way to deliver great content as well as to make sales, you don't want them to come across as scripted sales pitches, but instead as informational teleseminars that give listeners a chance to get more training from you.

Key Points

- Define your purpose for the teleseminar—selling coaching, building credibility, offering free consults, etc.
- Deliver incredible content and introduce the next step.
- Be intentional about asking prospects to take the next step, whether that is to purchase coaching, sign up for a free consult, or some other action step.

Recommended Training:

teleseminarselling.com
sellingcoaching.com

Get more at AnyoneCanCoach.net

Chapter 10

Sell Using a Sales Letter

Using a sales letter is the most efficient selling mechanism of all, as it can operate without your involvement, once created.

A coaching sales letter is a letter that tells your prospects about your coaching program and recommends that they sign up for it, and is the most efficient method of selling coaching. Although a sales letter doesn't "sell" as well as talking with someone personally over the phone, the advantage is that once you have written it, it continues to sell for you without any additional time investment. Your sales letter works daily, whether you do or not!

You can use the following basic instruction for writing a successful sales letter as a word-for-word guide; you can add to it, take away from it, or improve on it. If you choose to use it, you should improve on it over time by adding benefits and language that is unique to you and your coaching program. With that in mind, I'll show you how to write a basic sales letter for your coaching program or information package.

HEADLINE

The first thing your sales letter needs is a headline. A headline tells your reader what to expect in the letter, and is placed at the beginning. It is generally the first thing someone will read when he opens your letter, so it is important that the headline grabs your reader's attention so he will read the rest of the sales letter. If the headline doesn't grab your prospect's attention, he likely won't read your sales letter, and if he doesn't read your sales letter, he likely won't buy your program or package.

Your headline should either introduce the topic or results of your coaching, or create curiosity for your solution.

Here are some headline examples:

Discover the Secret to . . .

Revealed—the Secret to . . .

How to . . .

Do You Want to Discover How to . . .

Do You Want to Learn How to . . .

Discovered—The Best Way to . . .

Revealed—The Best Way to . . .

The Best Way to . . .

Are You Ready to . . .

OPEN THE SALES LETTER

The opening introduces yourself and identifies your audience. This might look like:

From: (Your Name)

To: You, IF you want to . . . (some result your prospect could achieve by working with you)

You can also name or list something (or multiple things) that might disqualify someone from working with you.

For example:

Note: This letter is not for you if . . .

. . . You are not wanting to improve (what you will help someone improve in your coaching).

. . . You are not willing to work hard to achieve results (success doesn't happen overnight, and if that's what you are looking for, I am not the right person for you).

. . . You aren't ready to make changes in your life.

While this works well to disqualify someone who is not right for your coaching, this can also serve as a takeaway that influences some prospects to want your coaching more. Some people will conclude that the change is not worth the effort, and they will disqualify themselves from working with you. Others will decide that they really do want to make the change in their lives, and that they're willing to take the necessary steps, even if it means some form of sacrifice or work to which they are not accustomed.

IDENTIFY THE FRUSTRATION (WHY SOMEONE NEEDS YOU)

The next section of your sales letter highlights the frustration or pain someone is experiencing as a result of his challenge or problem. If someone isn't experiencing frustration or pain as a result of his challenge or problem, it is unlikely he will feel like he needs you.

Here are some examples:

- *Are you frustrated with . . . (something that frustrates in your niche)?*

- *Have you been struggling with . . . (something people struggle with in your niche), and aren't (something folks in your niche should be achieving) like you should be?*

- *Have you been frustrated because you don't know what to do or how to do it to (something you teach in your program)?*

You can use about 3–5 of these (don't use too many) to uncover the struggles and frustration of most of the people who are reading your sales letter. These questions are designed to help prospects uncover and realize their pain and how much it is impacting them. You are helping them remember why they need a solution.

IDENTIFY WITH THE PAIN

In this section, identify with your prospect and his frustration, pain, or struggles. You can do this by writing about how prior or current clients experienced similar frustration, pain, or struggles before they started working with you; or you can present it from a personal point of view and write about how you identify with your prospect, because you experienced the same frustration, pain, or struggles before you discovered or learned what you will teach in your program.

Here are a few examples of identifying with your reader's pain:

If so, I understand, because when I first started, I didn't know how either. (You can tell your story about the kind of challenges you had before you discovered your solution, and how you have overcome your challenges.)

Or:

Some of my clients were in the same position when they started to work with me. They felt (a specific frustration) and were struggling to make the necessary changes.

Or a blend:

I understand, because when I first started I didn't know how either. (You can tell your story and the kind of challenges you had before you discovered your solution, and how you have overcome your challenges.)

And some of my clients were in the same position when they started to work with me, and just as the solution worked for me, it also worked for my clients. (You can tell how it worked for your clients.)

DIG DEEPER INTO THE FRUSTRATION WITH THE CHALLENGES OR PROBLEMS

Next, dig deeper into the frustration you've just drawn out or identified.

Here are some examples:

- *The bottom line is, it's time consuming to (something that is time consuming to do), especially if you don't know (something that not-knowing makes it time consuming), right?*

- *Sometimes you get frustrated with (something people get frustrated with in your niche), right?*

- *You feel like you are spinning your wheels, don't know what to do, and don't have the confidence to (something in your niche).*

- *Perhaps you've been working hard, trying to (some action people take in your niche) or maybe you even (some other action people take in your niche), but you don't know how to (something people in your niche commonly don't know how to do, or how to do well).*

- *Or maybe you have been working feverishly to (something people do in your niche), but you don't know what to do to (something that leads to something people do in your niche) and you know that if you don't (achieve what you just wrote), you aren't going to (name the achievement), right?*

- *Or maybe you have been (doing something people commonly do to get started in your niche), but now it is getting really hard to figure out (something that's hard to figure out in your niche), (something else that's hard to figure out in your niche), (something else that's hard to figure out in your niche), or (something else that's hard to figure out in your niche).*

You could conclude this section with something like this:

And those sound like simple problems . . . but you and I both know that any one of them can hold you back from (something in your niche that people need to achieve or do or accomplish), and make it seem like you are just wasting your time and your money (in your niche), right?

I mean, for all the work you have put into (your niche or goal), you should be (something people should be accomplishing in your niche), right?

The thing is, what you have been doing probably hasn't been working, and that's likely why you are reading this right now. Because you are looking for a solution, and you are ready to begin getting results, right?

TIE CHALLENGES TO YOUR SOLUTION

The next step is to tie your prospect's challenges to your solution. Someone must feel as though your solution is the answer to what is holding him back from achieving the result or goal he wants. There must be a clear link in his mind between the fact that his challenges are holding him back, and the fact that your solution will allow him to finally get the result he wants to achieve. You must do more than just name his problems and state your solution; you must lay out the path from his problems and challenges to your solution.

Here is an example:

I have discovered a solution to these challenges, and I have been using my solution for (time frame) and have literally tested it in real life dozens of different ways, and have continued to improve it until it is the very best solution on earth for (your niche problem).

I have discovered that (something you have discovered).

And that if you (something you can do in your niche to get results).

And furthermore, if you (something else to get results).

Look, if you are missing just ONE of the above steps, you are (the negative result, for example, "leaving money on the table," "shooting yourself in the proverbial foot," or "losing ground in [your niche]")!

And that's the purpose of this letter.

Because I want to show you what you are missing . . . and show you how you can get it all right so that you can (name the result or achievement you promise).

The bottom line is, if you aren't (something your prospect should be accomplishing), and you aren't (something else he should be accomplishing) . . . you are (some negative result he is getting in his life) every single day your system is not correct.

And I want to help you fix the leak so you can start (getting some result he will get with your system) instead of just spending money month after month to get (some false result he is getting/not getting now) that doesn't (something that doesn't work about the way he is doing it now).

Next, tell about your coaching program and how working with you will solve his challenges.

Here is an example:

So I have created a simple, step-by-step training program that literally walks you through every step of the way.

For the next 12 months (or any other time frame you want for your program), I am going to personally work with you to teach you EXACTLY how to (something you will teach) and (something else you will teach) so that you can start achieving (some result someone will get in working with you).

That's right—I have created a complete step-by-step training program that is 12 modules long. Each module comes with several hours of recorded teaching, PLUS a pdf homework assignment of exactly what to do and how to do it to get that part of your business up and running. And you will be held accountable for each step you complete (or don't complete).

Because all of these steps are necessary for you to (achieve the accomplishment or achievement you are going to teach how to do or achieve) next year.

So here is what you are going to learn:

* *How to (something you are going to teach)—no matter what (some objection you normally hear).*

* *My own personal method of determining EXACTLY (something you will teach to determine exactly in your niche).*

* *Step-by-step directions for (doing or achieving something you are going to teach).*

* *My super-easy (something you are going to teach) formula—I even GIVE you a sample (some sample you are going to give)—that you can EASILY customize for your (problem or niche). I even give you exact directions for that, as well—so you can (something your prospect will be able to accomplish).*

* *My never-before-revealed (something you haven't taught or revealed) formula for (something you are going to teach) . . . and how to make sure (someone doesn't make some common mistake), and how to (something your prospect needs to learn) quickly and easily.*

* *My own secret formula for (something you are going to teach) so that by (some time period) you have (some result) and (something cool about the result).*

* *How to know if you should (something your prospect needs to know if he should do or not do, preferably something your prospect is normally confused about).*

* *My brand new personal formula for (something you are going to teach), and (something else you are going to teach). This is a brand new teaching, never before revealed except to (a special group of your clients who already have this information).*

* *Additionally, I am going to teach you (something else you are going to teach), complete with (something else you are going to teach)—to literally (the result someone will get when he implements what you are going to teach) where you literally only have to (something simple someone has to do), and (some great result that happens when someone does that simple step).*

Write about the delivery method, value, and price. Explain why the training is worth what you charge, and suggest that your prospect sign up to work with you.

Here is an example:

So . . . how is this going to be delivered?

First, you are going to receive (however many hours or pages, etc., of content) of incredible teaching, exactly what you need to learn how to (accomplish what you are promising). (some dollar value, for example, $1,000 value)

Next, I am going to give you (some sample or template you are going to give). (some dollar value, for example, $1,000 value)

Next, I am going to include my (some time period) daily plan—this is a day-by-day, take-you-by-the-hand-and-show-you-how-its-done daily plan. (some dollar value, for example, $1,000 value)

You are also going to receive (some period of coaching access to you). (some dollar value, for example, $1,000 value)

And (some other method of coaching access to you or other delivery method). (some dollar value, for example, $1,000 value)

Plus you are going to receive: (name a bonus, possibly describe it briefly)

And another: (some other bonus) (some dollar value, for example, $1,000 value)

The total value of this training program is $6,000 . . . but today I am discounting this training to just $1,000, which is an 83% discount for you, because I want to make it a no-brainer for you to take action and change your life today.

(link to payment method)

PLUS—you are going to get to (something else someone is going to get to do with you)—AND you will get to ask me any questions you might have (as your prospect begins to do something that will implement your teaching or formula) using my formula.

In addition to my step-by-step system for (some result you are going to give) that works like clockwork, and that is easy to implement—and the exact system for (something you are teaching, for example, the end result) (including some hidden techniques many clients have never seen), you are also going to learn:

How to know EXACTLY (something you are going to teach how to do) and in WHICH order to do the steps to get the (some accomplishment your prospect wants to achieve, for example, most results).

You'll learn how to create (something your prospect will create).

You'll also learn how to know exactly what to (something your prospect will do) BEFORE (some achievement that needs to have the first thing done before it can be accomplished).

You'll also learn how to correctly (something you are going to teach) so that you achieve (some result your prospect will achieve when he implements what you are teaching). This is my own blended system I personally developed after studying many (things you have studied, e.g., systems, methods, etc.) . . . and my clients who have been exposed to this have been AMAZED.

How to create the precise balance between (two things in your niche that need balance).

Learn the BEST way to (something you are going to teach) . . . one of my techniques ensures you will achieve (some result you teach), while simultaneously achieving (some other result) . . . and you don't have to (something someone doesn't have to do to get results)!

Ok, are you ready now? Would it change your life if you had a 100% complete system like the one I use to (something your system teaches) . . . (something wonderful about your system)? As you know, (something cool you have done as a result of your system).

If so—I suggest you enroll in my new coaching program TODAY.

(link to payment method)

To make all of this easier to visualize and tie together, I've included the entire text of a sample letter containing the above content and samples, along with additional content and tie-ins. Feel free to use this as an example, copy any or all of it, or just start from scratch!

SALES LETTER SAMPLE:

"Are You Ready to Achieve (Result Your Prospect Could Achieve By Working With You)?"

From: (Your Name)

To: *You* IF you want to (some result your prospect could achieve by working with you)

Are you frustrated with (something that frustrates in your niche)?

Have you been struggling with (something that people struggle with in your niche), and aren't (something folks in your niche should be achieving) like you should be?

Sales Letter Sample (Continued)

Have you been frustrated because you don't know what to do or how to do it to (something you can teach someone to do in your program)?

If so, I understand, because when I first started I didn't know how either.

The bottom line is, it's time consuming to (something that is time consuming to do), especially if you don't know (something that not-knowing makes it time consuming), right?

Sometimes you get frustrated with (something people get frustrated with in your niche), right?

You feel like you are spinning your wheels, don't know what to do, and don't have the confidence you need to (something in your niche).

So what ELSE is holding you back from (the result you are going to teach someone to achieve), from being able to (something else you can help someone achieve)?

Perhaps you have been working hard, trying to (some action people take in your niche) or maybe you even (some other action people take in your niche), but you don't know how to (something people in your niche commonly don’t know how to do, or don’t know how to do well).

Sales Letter Sample (Continued)

Or maybe you have been working feverishly to (something people do in your niche) . . . but you don't know what to do to (something that leads to something people do in your niche) and you know that if you don't (achieve what you just wrote), you aren't going to (name the achievement), right?

Or maybe you have done (something people commonly do to get started in your niche), but now it is getting really confusing figuring out (something that's hard to figure out in your niche), (something else that's hard to figure out in your niche), (something else that's hard to figure out in your niche), or (something else that's hard to figure out in your niche).

And those sound like simple problems . . . but you and I both know that any one of them can hold you back from achieving (something in your niche that your prospect needs to achieve or do or accomplish), and make it seem like you are just wasting your time and your money (in your niche), right?

I mean, for all the work you have put into (your niche or goal), you should be (something your prospect should be accomplishing in your niche), right?

I think you should be!

Sales Letter Sample (Continued)

And my guess is that one of the problems I mentioned above is what's holding you back.

And the thing is, that's a lot like what held me back when I first got started.

(Tell about yourself here.

What you tried to accomplish.

How hard you tried.

All the things that failed.

How frustrated you were.

What happened.

Go into emotional detail here.)

And you can't (achieve some goal in your niche) (the way I was doing it).

(Write about why it won't work.

Anywhere from 3–12 sentences.)

So . . .

I was DETERMINED to (achieve your goal, name the goal).

Sales Letter Sample (Continued)

DETERMINED.

Just like you are.

So I began buying materials to teach me what to do and how to do it.

$97 here. $77 there. $197 somewhere else.

And none of them taught me everything I needed to know.

I studied them and was still stuck.

Ever feel that way?

I did.

I also tried (something else people try in your niche).

And it didn't work for me.

And here's why it didn't work for me:

(tell why it didn't work for you)

Just like it isn't working for you.

Then I discovered a HUGE secret.

Sales Letter Sample (Continued)

Frankly, I got so fed up with doing things the way everybody else was trying to do them, and failing every time, that I simply had to create my own solution.

So I set out to create my own solution. And it wasn't easy. It was a lot harder than I thought it would be.

I had to hire 5 experts to consult me, and I had to commission 3 different people to design a solution that would work.

And when they created the solution, I tested it, and tweaked it, and even threw out some parts of it, and demanded that the experts redesign parts of it, because it wasn't working the way I wanted it to.

And that was a frustrating process all by itself.

However . . . the good news is, that after (some dollar number) of investment, and (some number of hours) of time, and much frustration and angst, I finally had a fully operational solution in my hand that finally WORKED.

And I have been using my solution for (time frame) and have literally tested it in real life dozens of different ways, and have continued to improve it until it is the very best solution on earth for (your niche problem).

Sales Letter Sample (Continued)

This is the ONE thing the (experts in your niche, call them what they are called in your niche, experts, gurus, masters, winners, etc.) just don't want you to know.

Because they don't want everyone doing it.

But I am willing to show you.

First of all—why?

Because (give one reason why you are willing to show it to your prospect).

Because it just isn't fair for you to continue (not achieving the goal) . . . when I have the answer.

And I do.

And I have the proof.

Because I have personally used this answer for the last (your time frame in months or years [whatever is accurate and true]).

My first (period, e.g., month or year) I achieved (some accomplishment) once I started using this secret.

Each year since I have (minimum achievement since first period).

Sales Letter Sample (Continued)

And I don't tell you that to brag.

And I don't tell you that to promise you can (do exactly the same thing).

Because I can't.

Because I don't know how hard you will work (I worked HARD).

And I don't know if you will only use half my system and try to do the rest on your own because you think your way works better.

Look, I know that might have sounded rude . . . but I've seen it time and time again.

People buy a system, and think they can improve on it before they have (made some accomplishment in your niche) . . . and then fail. And then blame the system. And that's just not right, is it?

So I want you to promise me that if I reveal my secret . . . you PROMISE to either use my entire system the way I teach it, and send me a thank you letter or testimonial afterwords . . . or just don't try my system at all. Fair enough? Promise?

Ok—here it is.

And before I give it to you—let me warn you.

Sales Letter Sample (Continued)

This is going to sound REALLY simple.

Like—why didn't I think of that?

And there are a lot of details that frankly if you don't get them right . . . my system won't work.

Ok—here it is:

I have discovered that (something you have discovered).

And that if you (something you can do in your niche to get results).

And furthermore, if you (something else to get results).

Look, if you are missing just ONE of the above steps, you are (the negative result, for example, "leaving money on the table," "shooting yourself in the proverbial foot," or "losing ground in [your niche]")!

And that's the purpose of this letter.

Because I want to show you what you are missing . . . and show you how you can get it all right so that you can (name the result or achievement you promise).

Sales Letter Sample (Continued)

The bottom line is, if you aren't (something your prospect should be accomplishing), and you aren't (something else he should be accomplishing) . . . *you are (some negative result he is getting in his life) every single day your system is not correct.*

And I want to help you fix the leak so you can start (some result your prospect will get with your system) instead of just spending money month after month to get (some false result he is getting/not getting now) that doesn't (something that doesn't work about the way he is doing it now).

So I have created a simple, step-by-step training program that literally walks you through every step of the way.

For the next 12 months (or any other time frame you want for your program), I am going to personally work with you to teach you EXACTLY how to (something you will teach in the program) and (something else you will teach) so that you can start (some result someone will get in working with you).

That's right—I have created a complete step-by-step training program that is 12 modules long. Each module comes with several hours of recorded teaching, PLUS a pdf homework assignment of exactly what to do and how to do it to get that part of your business up and running.

Sales Letter Sample (Continued)

And you will be held accountable for each step you complete (or don't complete). Because all of these steps are necessary for you to (the accomplishment or achievement you are going to teach) next year.

So here is what you are going to learn:

* How to (something you are going to teach)—no matter what (some objection you normally hear).

* My own personal method of determining EXACTLY (something you will teach your prospect to determine exactly in your niche).

* Step-by-step directions for (something you are going to teach).

* My super-easy (something you are going to teach) formula—I even GIVE you a sample (some sample you are going to give)—that you can EASILY customize for your (problem or niche). I even give you exact directions for that, as well—so you can (something your prospect will be able to accomplish).

* My never-before-revealed (something you haven't taught or revealed) formula for (something you are going to teach) . . . and how to make sure (your prospect doesn't make some common mistake), and how to (something he needs to learn) quickly and easily.

Sales Letter Sample (Continued)

* My own secret formula for (something you are going to teach in your program) so that by (some time period) you have (some result) and (something cool about the result).

* How to know if you should (something your prospect needs to know if he should do or not do, preferably something your prospects are normally confused about).

* My brand new personal formula for (something you are going to teach), and (something else you are going to teach). This is a brand new teaching, never before revealed except to (a special group of your clients who already have this information).

* **Additionally, I am going to teach you (something else you are going to teach), complete with (something else you are going to teach)—to literally (the result someone will get when he implements what you are going to teach) where you literally only have to (something simple someone has to do), and (some great result that happens when he does that simple step).**

So . . . how is this going to be delivered?

First, you are going to receive (however many hours or pages, etc., of content) of incredible teaching, exactly what you need to learn how to (accomplish what you are promising). (some dollar value, for example, $1,000 value)

Sales Letter Sample (Continued)

Next, I am going to give you (some sample or template you are going to give). (some dollar value, for example, $1,000 value)

Next, I am going to include my (some time period) daily plan—this is a day-by-day, take-you-by-the-hand-and-show-you-how-its-done daily plan. (some dollar value, for example, $1,000 value)

(Some period of coaching access to you) (some dollar value, for example, $1,000 value)

(Some other method of coaching access to you or other delivery method) (some dollar value, for example, $1,000 value)

Bonus: (name the bonus, possibly describe it briefly)

Bonus: (some other bonus) (some dollar value, for example, $1,000 value)

PLUS—you are going to get to (something else your prospect is going to get to do with you)—AND you will get to ask me any questions you might have (as he begins to do something that will implement your teaching or formula) using my formula.

So perhaps you are wondering, is this for me?

First let me say this . . . this is NOT for you if:

Sales Letter Sample (Continued)

You are NOT willing to (something someone must be willing to do to get results, for example, work hard). You see, it is a (something that your system is), and I teach you exactly what to do and how to do it—but you have to do the beginning work to (get some result).

You are a (something that describes some trait that won't work with your system, for example, lazy person).

You are not willing to follow directions.

You want someone to hand you a free lunch.

If any of the above describes you—this program is NOT for you.

But if you are the kind of person:

Who is willing to work hard for (some time period, for example, 3–6 months) while you learn what works and get things set up.

Who really wants to (some accomplishment you are going to teach your client to achieve) and won't stop until you get there.

Who really wants to get my secrets and formulas rather than stumbling around for the next 2–3 years trying to figure it all out on your own . . .

Then this probably IS for you.

Sales Letter Sample (Continued)

Of course YOU have to make the decision.

In addition to my step-by-step system for (some result you are going to give to your client) that works like clockwork, and that is easy to implement—and the exact system for (something you are teaching, for example, the end result) (including some hidden techniques many clients have never seen), you are also going to learn:

1. How to know EXACTLY (something you are going to teach how to do) and in WHICH order to get the (some accomplishment your prospect wants to achieve, for example, most results).

2. How to create (something your prospect will create).

3. How to know exactly what to (something he will do) BEFORE (some achievement that needs to occur first).

4. How to correctly (something you are going to teach in the program) so that you are (some result he will get when he implements what you are teaching). This is my own blended system I personally developed after studying many (things you have studied, e.g., systems, methods, etc.) . . . and my clients who have been exposed to this have been AMAZED.

5. How to create the precise balance between (two things in your niche that need balance).

Sales Letter Sample (Continued)

6. Learn the BEST way to (something you are going to teach) . . . one of my techniques ensures you will achieve (some result you teach), while simultaneously achieving (some other result) . . . and you don't (something someone doesn't have to do to get results)!

Ok, are you ready now? Would it change your life if you had a 100% complete system like the one I use to (something your system teaches) . . . (something wonderful about your system or result)? As you know, (something cool you have done as a result of your system).

If so—I suggest you enroll in my new coaching program TODAY.

Let's review everything you will get:

First, you are going to receive (however many hours or pages, etc., of content) of incredible teaching, exactly what you need to learn how to (accomplish what you are promising). (some dollar value, for example, $1,000 value)

Next, I am going to give you (some sample or template you are going to include). (some dollar value, for example, $1,000 value)

Next, I am going to include my (some time period) daily plan—this is a day-by-day, take-you-by-the-hand-and-show-you-how-its-done daily plan. (some dollar value, for example, $1,000 value)

Sales Letter Sample (Continued)

(Some period of coaching access to you) (some dollar value, for example, $1,000 value)

(Some other method of coaching access to you or other delivery method) (some dollar value, for example, $1,000 value)

Bonus: (name the bonus, possibly describe it briefly)

Bonus: (some other bonus) (some dollar value, for example, $1000 value)

The total value of this training program is $6,000 . . .

but today I am discounting this training to just $1,000, which is an 83% discount for you, because I want to make it a no-brainer for you to take action and change your life today.

And frankly, I don't know how long I'll be able to leave this offer up, as (some reason why you might not be able to keep this offer up) . . .

So I suggest if you are serious about (accomplishing something in your niche) that you take action now and get into my new program before you are locked out:

(link to payment method)

(Your Signature and Name)

Sales Letter Sample (Continued)

P.S. Perhaps you are thinking (something someone in your niche thinks when he is thinking about not taking action).

And I understand why you might think that.

Because other people have thought that before, even some of my clients might have thought that before they signed up to work with me.

But now they are glad that they didn't let that hold them back, just like you will be.

So I suggest that you simply take control of your future, and make the right decision to begin controlling your future by finally getting on the right path to (some accomplishment you will teach your client to achieve).

Go ahead, take action now and enroll while you still can:

(link to payment method)

You can use that sample sales letter as a word-for-word guide or you can add to it, take away from it, or improve on it. If you choose to use it, either as a guide or as is, you should improve on it over time by adding benefits and language that is unique to you and your coaching program.

Once you have written your sales letter, you can include it in your email campaign on a regular basis, and people can enroll without your active involvement. It's something you can literally create once and it continues to work for you month after month and year after year. And over time, you can improve it, adding to it as you learn new ways to persuade through writing.

When you first get started with coaching, the sales letter is less important than it will be in the future, because initially you will primarily be using one-on-one calls to enroll clients. Because of that, you don't want to spend a lot of time on your sales letter right up front, but long-term, the more you can learn about sales letter writing and persuasive writing, the more effective your sales letters will become.

Key Points

- Your sales letter generally contains a targeted and exciting headline.
- Include one or more opening paragraphs, introducing you, introducing an idea, or introducing typical prospects' challenges.
- List or describe typical prospects' challenges.
- Identify the pain associated with those challenges.
- Tie those challenges to your solution.
- Explicitly offer your solution and make it easy for your prospect to take action.

Recommended Reading:

The Ultimate Sales Letter by Dan Kennedy

Recommended Resources:

coachsalesletterwriting.com
marlonsalesletters.com (sales letter software by Marlon Sanders)

Get more at AnyoneCanCoach.net

Chapter 11

Additional Revenue Streams

In addition to providing coaching, you can also create and sell information products such as books, home-study courses, and audio programs that serve as additional learning materials for clients and additional revenue for you.

In addition to your coaching program(s), you can add additional revenue and value to your coaching business by creating and selling information products such as audio- or video-training programs and home-study courses.

You could start by creating a basic introductory-level information product that teaches the topics in the master outline that you created based on the instructions on pages 29–31. Once you have created the basic introductory training, you could create additional deeper-level training programs based on each sub-topic from your master outline. In the long run, as you gain prospects and clients, you can ask them what their challenges are, and then create products that address and solve those challenges.

Your information product can either be written, audio, or video in format. An audio series is generally the easiest to produce, since speaking takes less time than writing, and recording audio takes less time than recording video. In addition, unless your topic specifically needs to be visually illustrated, video generally doesn't add much value to your client's experience (in fact, it is usually easier for your client to listen to an audio; for example, on the way to work, while doing housework, or while multitasking online; than to sit and watch a video). If there are some parts that need video for illustrative purposes, but most of the material can be taught with audio, then video-record only the portions that specifically need it, and use audio for everything else. As a result, your product will be more useful. Your clients will be more likely to use the training, which means they are more likely to get the results they desire.

OUTLINE YOUR INFORMATION PRODUCT

Create a detailed outline of everything you know and want to teach about the topic of your information product. It should contain at least 8 (preferably 10–12) primary ideas or topics. Under each topic, create additional sub-topics. These can be things that need to be taught to fully understand the topic or idea itself, or these might be ordered steps to accomplishing the result. (This process is identical to the "10 x 10 matrix" concept I shared on pages 29–31 about creating an outline for your coaching program.)

Your completed outline should look something like the following generic outline:

Topic 1

Sub-topic 1

Sub-topic 2

Sub-topic 3

. . . and so on, through at least 8, but preferably 10–12 sub-topics.

Topic 2

Sub-topic 1

Sub-topic 2

Sub-topic 3

. . . and so on . . .

Topic 3

Sub-topic 1

Sub-topic 2

Sub-topic 3

. . . and so on . . .

Topics 4-10, with 8-12 sub-topics each.

When this is completed, you should have about 100 sub-topics (8–12 topics X 8–12 sub-topics).

RECORD THE AUDIO OR VIDEO SERIES (HOME-STUDY COURSE)

The first step is to choose what software you will use to record your training. Your computer may come pre-installed with audio- or video-recording software, and you can use that. If not, there is downloadable or online-based software you can purchase, and I've listed the ones I currently use here: recommendedteleseminars.com. For video, when you want to record your computer screen (for showing slides, etc.), I recommend camtasia.com if you use a pc, or screenflow.com if you use a mac. If you are recording something offline, I recommend using a video recorder that is designed for easy uploading to the web (I hesitate to recommend a brand, as you will likely want to purchase the most advanced video recorder currently available, and that will change over time).

The next step is the actual recording. Using your outline as a guide, simply teach aloud your expertise. This is simpler than it may sound if you've never done it before, so my advice is to just try it. You will likely be amazed at how easy it is.

Think of it this way: If you are using the 10 x 10 matrix outline you created earlier with 100 sub-topics, and teach for only 6 minutes on each sub-topic, that's 10 sub-topics an hour. With 100 sub-topics that is a total of 10 hours of home-study teaching. 6 minutes is not a lot of time to teach on any one sub-topic! And of course, it doesn't have to be 6 minutes . . . some sub-topics will take longer than others to teach, some won't take as long. It's not important. What is important is the information itself, not how long it takes to teach.

WRITE AN ACCOMPANYING MANUAL

You can add value to your information product by writing an accompanying supporting manual. This manual might summarize the main points in your product; offer additional tips or resources; or contain links to supporting documents, tools, or additional products. Write the manual as concisely and as well-organized as possible so that it will get the most use and deliver the most value to your client.

Use a word processor for writing the manual, then convert the finished document into a pdf for distribution. Your word processor likely contains an easy way to convert the document into a pdf, but if it does not, I recommend acrobat.com/createpdf.

DELIVER YOUR INFORMATION PRODUCT

Once your product is created, upload it to your website and create a web page from which your client can download the training (this is commonly called a download page). For example, if you record a 10-mp3-series product, create a download page that has 10 links: one link to each mp3. When someone purchases the product, send him the download page through your autoresponder; I list the ones I use here: recommendedautoresponders.com. You may also be able to send the download page directly from the merchant service you use to collect payment, or you can use a shopping cart to send the download page.

The next step in the process of creating your products is to create a sales letter for each product, just as you created one for your coaching program. You can use a similar format to the one I taught you in Chapter 10 for writing a coaching sales letter, or you can use a sales letter creator such as marlonsalesletters.com. (I recommend using a sales page creator for writing your product sales letters if you are just getting started; the time investment in learning to write product sales letters is likely not worth it for your first few products. Your time is probably better spent generating prospects, talking with them in free consults, and coaching clients.)

CREATE MULTIPLE PRODUCTS (SALES FUNNEL)

Now that you have created one product, how many more could you create? Could you create a product for each of the topics you brainstormed in the beginning of this section?

Could you create multiple products on each topic? For example, could you create a 2- to 3-hour introductory- or intermediate-level audio teaching, and a more-advanced 10-hour audio teaching? Could you create a monthly continuity program where subscribers get one new teaching per month for some number of months (for example, instead of 10 hours in a single product, you could have a 10-month program, where the buyer gets one hour per month delivered via email)? Or could you create a new 10-hour home-study course each quarter? As you grow your business, you will find that some clients will purchase nearly everything you produce, so the more you produce, the more you sell (in addition to building a great product line to complement your coaching).

SAMPLE PRODUCT FUNNEL STRUCTURES

Here are a few samples of how you could structure your product funnel:

Sample 1:

6-month coaching program
10-hour home-study course
5-hour entry-level mp3 series
Several 1-hour mp3 teachings

Sample 2:

3-month coaching program
12-month coaching program
20-hour home-study course
8-hour home-study course
A book
Several 1- to 2-hour audio programs

Sample 3:

8-week coaching program
Open-ended (monthly) coaching program
Multiple home-study courses (varying in length between 8 hours and 20 hours each)
Multiple single-hour audios
Multiple books

As you can see, with just a little imagination, you could create any combination of products and coaching programs you want. There is no "perfect" product funnel structure; instead, focus on producing products and coaching programs that meet your clients' needs and you will find that your product funnel "produces itself" over time!

Key Points

- You can create additional information products such as ebooks, audio programs, and home-study courses for additional revenue and to provide additional learning opportunities for your clients.
- You can integrate these additional products into an organized, coherent sales funnel.
- You can integrate your sales funnel with your coaching program(s) to create the deepest level of client involvement at all price points and demographics within your niche.

Recommended Reading:

The Official Get Rich Guide to Information Marketing by Dan Kennedy, Bill Glazer, and Robert Skrob

Additional Resources:

infobusinessautomation.com
blackbeltsalesfunnel.com
recommendedteleseminars.com
marlonsalesletters.com

Get more at AnyoneCanCoach.net

Chapter 12

Build Trust Through Email

To build a natural trusting relationship with your prospects efficiently over time, write a relationship building email campaign that will deliver content and build trust over time on autopilot.

Before someone makes a decision to join your coaching program, he must grow to trust you and believe that you can help him. This occurs through a natural process of emotional and psychological actions and triggers called primal bonding. Offline, this tends to happen when we spend time with, interact with, and communicate with someone over time.

For example, when you first begin to build a relationship offline, you might meet for coffee and share a few ideas. Then a few days later you might meet for lunch, and share some more thoughts. Perhaps you continue meeting for lunch or coffee, and talk on the phone from time to time.

As you continue to spend time with someone offline, you tend to develop trust and rapport with that individual. If it is a professional relationship, that person might feel drawn to you because he sees that you have a level of authority in the professional area in which he is engaged. All of these interactions allow the offline relationship to grow slowly over time, creating a strong primal bond.

The same thing happens when you are building trust with an online prospect, except that you are meeting through email, teleseminars, and sales letters, rather than at lunch, coffee, and over the phone.

When someone joins your list, you begin the process of primal bonding, and you create and deepen trust and connection over time. Patience is key here, because it takes time for your prospect to trust and respect you. You'll begin to have a sense of when someone is ready for your coaching, and she will be easier to enroll in your coaching because of the long-term relationship you have built with her. You can enroll clients with more ease this way than if you try to sell them too fast using other models.

You might be asking . . . well, isn't it a lot of work, writing these emails, and communicating and building these relationships? Well . . . yes . . . and no. Here's why: When you use email marketing to help build these relationships, you will be using an email autoresponder, which is a software-driven service that allows you to send a series of relationship-building emails automatically to each subscriber who joins your list. Your autoresponder will send each email in your series to each subscriber on your list, sequentially over time; each email will be sent a specified number of days after the subscriber has joined your list. This means that you could write a series of, for example, 100 emails, and schedule those emails to each go out to each subscriber, for example, every 3rd day after that subscriber has joined your list.

These emails are personalized, and although many prospects realize they are sent automatically, the emails still help them to begin to feel as though they are bonding directly with you. This is especially true when someone responds to one of these emails, asks you a question, and you personally respond to that email. That psychologically strengthens the primal bond between you and your prospect, and prospects begin to read the emails as if they were written just for them.

Also, by sending prospects a series of emails about you, your coaching, and your systems, over time, instead of allowing your prospects to consume the information all in one sitting on your website, you are able to mimic offline relationship building. It also allows you to control what someone receives from you, and in what order, thus controlling the psychological process necessary to build trust, rapport, and confidence in you.

WRITE A PRIMAL BONDING EMAIL CAMPAIGN

The primary purpose of your email campaign is to build trust and relationship, creating the primal bonding connection; the secondary purpose is to inspire prospects to enroll in your coaching program or buy your products. The most efficient way to create the primal bonding experience online is to use a long-term perpetual email campaign that continually engages with your prospects, and is completely automated.

You might start with an initial "credibility push" the first 10 days someone is enrolled in your campaign, with an email each day for the first 10 days; then taper to an email every other day through the rest of the first month. For the second and third months, you might taper to one email every third day, and after three months, you might go to one email every fourth or fifth day. After six months, you might taper this to once every seven to ten days.

I recommend writing out the first three to six months of emails ahead of time, then adding future emails as needed. For example, you might initially write 100 emails for your campaign, and this might cover 6 months. Then you could write 1 email per week and add it to the end of your campaign, and as prospects move through your campaign, they will always be receiving an additional email every 7 to 10 days.

There are 2 primary categories into which your emails will generally tend to fall:

- Content-based emails (emails with valuable information about your niche, links to articles, or links to videos or audios)

- Sales-based emails (emails actively selling or recommending the purchase of your products or enrolling in coaching)

There are several things you will want to achieve purposefully as you write the emails. Initially, your core goal will be to build trust and credibility in your campaign by writing content-based emails. Over time, you will continue to build on this base of trust and credibility with additional content-based emails, but you will also want to create emails that move people towards enrolling in your coaching or buying your products.

Maintain a balance between content-based emails and sales-based emails. If you send only content, you won't make many sales or enroll many clients. But if you send only sales-based emails, your prospects will quickly unsubscribe and no longer be prospects. I recommend using a 2:1 balance of content to sales emails, meaning that you write 2 content-based emails for every 1 sales-based email.

These emails won't necessarily always be in exactly that ratio in the short run, but should approximate that over time. For example, you may have a segment in your campaign that has 6 content-based emails leading to a coaching program launch sequence of 4 sales-based emails, followed by 2 content-based emails.

There isn't a one-size-fits-all sequence of emails that will get the best results. Your email campaign will vary based on your own writing style, the needs of your prospects, and what you have to offer. You may want to offer much more free content with fewer calls to action, and keep prospects in your campaign much longer; or you may prefer to be more aggressive and generate clients faster, and in the process, lose some prospects who might have converted into clients over a longer period of time. Neither strategy is right or wrong, but rather, is better or worse for you, based on your preferences or style. Here are some types of emails you might write:

Content-based emails:

- Containing a tip or idea your prospects can use.
- Containing a link to an article you have written.
- Containing a link to useful information you have found online.
- Containing a link to an audio you have recorded.
- Containing a link to a video you have created.

Sales-based emails:

- Containing a link to a sales letter for your coaching program.
- Containing a link to a sales letter for a product or home-study course you have created.
- Containing an application to enroll in your coaching program.

- Containing an invite to talk with you personally in a free consult.
- Inviting your prospect to a teleseminar you will be holding.

Here is a sample campaign:

Day 1: email introducing yourself, with a link to your website, blog, or coaching program

Day 2: email with a link to an article you have written

Day 3: email with a link to a video you have recorded (perhaps a 5 minute video teaching a topic in your niche)

Day 4: email with a link to apply for your coaching program

Day 5: email with a link to an audio you have recorded

Day 6: email with a tip relevant to your prospects' typical challenges

Day 7: email with a link to purchase a home-study course

Day 8: email with content (perhaps a link to an article that has been published on a niche website)

Day 9: email with content (perhaps a link to a video)

Day 10: email with more content.

Day 11 might be a great time to send out an email asking for the prospect to reply with her challenges, initiating the email exchange I describe on pages 121-126 that culminates in inviting her to a free consult. Your prospects have had enough time to get to know and trust you to some extent, but it has not been so long that they have found another solution from someone else.

At this point, you could begin a long-term campaign, rotating content and sales messages. In the following example, I will assume you have a coaching program and 3 home-study courses, so you will be promoting those courses and your coaching program, and presenting content in your email campaign. Following your 10-day entry campaign, your continuing campaign might look like this:

Day 11: "I need your help" email (modeled in the "free consult" section on pages 122-123)

Day 14: content-based email

Day 16: content-based email

Day 18: email introducing a home-study course

Day 20: email with more information about your home-study course

Day 22: email asking if readers have questions about your home-study course

Day 24: content-based email

Day 26: content-based email

Day 28: content-based email

Day 30: repeat "I need your help" email (It's been 30 days total; some prospects who weren't "warmed up" enough to respond on day 11 may be ready now.)

Day 35: content-based email

Day 38: content-based email

Day 41: introduce second home-study course

Day 44: more info on second home-study course

Day 47: questions and answers about your second home-study course

Day 50: content-based email

Day 55: content-based email

Day 60: sales letter for coaching program

Day 65: "I need your help" email

Day 70: content-based email

Day 75: content-based email

Day 80: introduction to third home-study course

Day 85: more information about third home-study course

Day 90: still more information about third home-study course

Day 95: content-based email

Day 100: content-based email

As you can see, this has begun to set a pattern that can be repeated time and again. After 100 days of content in your campaign, you can easily continue it indefinitely by just writing 1–2 emails a week, and adding them to the end of the campaign. For example, in this scenario, the next 2 emails might go out on days 105 and 110.

By keeping in touch by delivering quality content, you will keep yourself in the forefront of your prospects' minds so that when they need the kind of help you provide, they will think of you first. When you are ready to market a new coaching program, re-market an old one, launch a new product, or simply look for new clients, you will have a responsive list of prospects to talk with.

The key is to not only make sales, but to also build relationships with your subscribers. If someone writes and asks a question, write back personally or have someone on your staff do so. Very few people will ask questions through email, but if you respond to the few who write, they will instantly upgrade their trust and opinion of you. And future autoresponder emails will feel even more personal to those subscribers with whom you have personally communicated.

HOW TO WRITE A CONTENT-BASED EMAIL

The purpose of the content-based email is to deliver content to the subscriber. This can be done by including the content in the email itself, or by recommending a link that leads to the content.

Here is an example of the format of an email with the content included in the email:

Content Included in the Email:

Subject Line:

(Prospect Name) — A Tip Regarding (Topic of Tip)

Body:

(Prospect Name), here is a tip for you:

Write out the information, this could be a few lines or a few paragraphs, depending on the depth of what you are sharing. I recommend varying the length of these emails. People don't tend to regularly read long emails, although sometimes a longer email can more effectively share the information. So although you might occasionally write a longer email (more than 500 words, for example), the bulk of your emails should be in the 200-300 words-or-less range.

To your success,

(Your Name)

Here is an example of the format of an email with the content linked-to in the email:

Content Linked-to in the Email:

Subject Line:

(Prospect Name) — A Tip Regarding (Topic of Tip)

Body:

(Prospect Name),

Here is some information regarding (topic of tip) that I think will be helpful to you:

(link to content; for example, link to article, link to website with information, etc.)

I hope this helps!

(Your Name)

You can use the same type of email for delivering a link to an audio or a video tip, or for delivering any other kind of content or information. I've been known to use that style of email to announce a new article I've written, a new website

I've launched, or even to showcase a client's work (which enhances my own credibility).

Here is an example of showcasing a client's work:

Email Showcasing a Client's Work:

Subject Line:

(Prospect Name) — Results from one of my clients

Body:

(Prospect Name),

Yesterday I received an email from one of my clients, sharing with me the results she has received in working with me. I was so excited about it that I asked her if I could share it with you; I think you will love this: (content of email)

I hope you get as much out of this as I did!

(Your Name)

Of course, you could recommend a link instead of copying an email, for example, something like this:

A client recently completed a new sales page and I thought I would share it with you: (link to sales page)

Or:

One of my clients recently wrote an article that was featured in (some magazine) and I thought I would share it with you: (link to article)

Obviously, there are a limitless number of ways you could share content, but I hope this gives you some idea of not only what types of things you can send, but also how creative you can be. Anything that could be of value to someone on your list, or that could enhance the learning experience for someone on your list, could be a good choice to send to your subscribers.

HOW TO WRITE A SALES-BASED EMAIL

As with writing content-based emails, there are a limitless number of ways you can write a sales-based email. One is with a link-oriented email, where you simply recommend someone go to a sales page. Another is with an email that tells a story, builds suspense or heightens desire, or otherwise stimulates interest in whatever you are selling, then recommends an action.

Here are two examples:

Email Recommending a Sales Page:

Subject Line:

(Prospect Name) — How to Get (Some Results)

Body:

(Prospect Name),

How would you like to get (some result)?

If that would be exciting to you, I recommend you check this out: (link to sales page of product or sales page of coaching program)

(Your Name)

Email Recommending a Sales Page (more advanced):

Subject Line:

(Prospect Name) — How to (Get Some Result)

Body:

(Prospect Name), do you want to (get some result)?

Do you get frustrated because you have tried (something) or (something else) and just aren't getting the results you want?

Or maybe you have (something people do unsuccessfully in your niche to get results) and it just isn't working out?

The thing is, it isn't easy (getting some result).

But I have created a solution I think you should consider: (link to sales page with solution)

(Your Name)

PRODUCT OR COACHING LAUNCH SEQUENCE

You can also stage a succession of emails building to and supporting the sale of your product or coaching program.

This might look like a series of emails that sequentially does the following:

1. identifies prospect frustration
2. builds on frustration and enhances awareness of pain
3. enhances desire for solution
4. announces upcoming solution
5. releases solution
6. sends additional information about solution
7. sends additional information about solution (again)
8. creates pressure or utilizes scarcity regarding solution
9. gives a final chance to obtain solution (if solution is time-based, for example, a coaching program with a fixed enrollment date)

Here are examples of each of those emails (using a new coaching program as an example):

Email That Identifies Prospect Frustration:

Subject Line:

(Prospect Name) — Are you Frustrated By (Something in Your Niche That Frustrates and Is Solved In Your Coaching Program)?

Body:

(Prospect Name),

Do you ever get frustrated by (something that frustrates)?

How about (something else that frustrates)?

How much is (the frustration) holding you back from getting the results you want?

(Your Name)

Email That Builds on Frustration and Enhances Awareness of Pain:

Subject Line:

(Prospect Name) — How Much is (Some Frustration) Holding You Back?

Body:

(Prospect Name),

If you are anything like me, when you experience (some frustration) it holds you back from (some result).

It feels like (example) or maybe like (another example).

The thing is, it's not a pleasant feeling (the way someone feels with the frustration).

So let me ask you this . . . deep down inside, how would it feel to overcome (the frustration)?

What would be the result for you of overcoming (the frustration)?

How would your life change?

How would it feel to have those life changes?

(Your Name)

Email That Enhances Desire For Solution:

Subject Line:

(Prospect Name) — What Happens When You Overcome (Frustration)

Body:

(Prospect Name),

Yesterday we talked about how it would feel to overcome (frustration).

The thing is, (your frustration) is holding you back from (list what it is holding the subscriber back from).

And without changing that, you are going to continue to experience (frustration).

I am in the process of putting the final touches on a new coaching program that is going to show you (name three ways your coaching program will relieve your subscriber's frustration).

So let me ask you this: How would it feel to overcome (the frustration) by (summarize the three ways mentioned in the last paragraph)?

(Your Name)

Email Announcing Upcoming Solution:

Subject Line:

(Prospect Name) — Get the Results You Desire!

Body:

(Prospect Name),

As I mentioned a few days ago, I've been putting the final touches on a brand new coaching program to help you (whatever the coaching program will help with).

Finally, tomorrow is the big day!

I wanted to let you know ahead of time, because I have decided to make this coaching program really personal, so I'm limiting it to just 10 people, which is going to allow me to really work with you personally.

Now, the announcement email tomorrow is going to go out to ([size of your list] people, for example, 500 people) who are looking for a solution to (the frustration solved by your coaching program), so my guess is that the 10 slots will go fast.

All of that to say . . . if you want to solve your (frustration) once and for all, be looking for the email from me tomorrow at (some time, for example, 10 AM EST).

I look forward to working with you!

(Your Name)

Email That Releases Solution:

Subject Line:

(Prospect Name) — Announcing my Brand New (Name of Coaching Program)

Body:

(Prospect Name),

As promised, I've just opened the doors to my brand new coaching program, (Name of Coaching Program).

Read all about it here: (link to coaching program sales letter)

(Your Name)

Email That Sends Additional Information About Solution:

Subject Line:

(Prospect Name) — Finally Conquer (Something In Your Niche)

Body:

(Prospect Name),

How would it feel to finally overcome (something frustrating in your niche)?

Or how about if you could (something else someone will accomplish in your coaching program)?

You'll achieve all of that and more in my brand new coaching program (Name of Coaching Program):

(link to coaching program sales letter)

(Prospect Name), I look forward to working with you!

(Your Name)

Email That Sends Additional Information About Solution (Again):

Subject Line:

(Prospect Name) — FAQ about my new coaching program . . .

Body:

(Prospect Name),

As you know, I have opened the doors to my new coaching program, and (some accurate number, for example, 6) people have enrolled so far, so there are only 4 slots left.

However, a number of people have asked some questions about the program, so I thought I would answer them here in case you are wondering the same things.

(Question 1)

Answer: (answer the question)

(Question 2)

Answer: (answer the question)

Are you ready to get signed up now? If so . . . do it here: (link to coaching program sales letter)

(Question 3)

Answer: (answer the question)

(Question 4)

Answer: (answer the question)

Are you ready to get signed up now? If so . . . do it here: (link to coaching program sales letter)

Keep in mind, there are only 4 spots available and this email has gone out to (accurate number, for example, 500) people and once the spots are gone . . . they are gone.

(Your Name)

Email That Creates Pressure or Utilizes Scarcity Regarding Solution:

Subject Line:

(Prospect Name) — 2 Spots Left

Body:

(Prospect Name),

Well, 2 more clients have signed up to work with me personally over the next 12 weeks, and that means there are 2 spots left.

The thing is, this is going to be a great training, and I don't want to see you miss out.

If you are serious about changing (some frustration or something else related to your coaching program), I suggest you consider getting involved before the last spots are taken: (link to coaching program sales letter)

I look forward to working with you!

(Your Name)

Email That Gives a Final Chance to Obtain Solution (if solution is time-based, for example, a coaching program with a fixed enrollment date):

Subject Line:

(Prospect Name) — Your Final Chance to Enroll

Body:

(Prospect Name),

Well, I guess most good things come to an end at some time . . . and this is one of those times. As you know, my brand new coaching program starts tomorrow, and so far 9 people have enrolled, so that means one spot is left.

So . . . if you have been thinking you want to make these changes in your life, but have been . . . procrastinating a little . . . there isn't any more time!

In fact, because I want to keep this program personal, I am capping it at 10 people, so if you are the 11th person to enroll, I will have to send your payment back.

So . . . if this is right for you, don't miss out, get signed up now! (link to coaching program sales letter)

(Your Name)

Obviously those are sample emails, and of course each campaign you write will be different. You might not want to use as much pressure as I've demonstrated in those samples! Or you might want to include more content in the campaign, answer more (or less) questions, etc.

Each campaign should not only feel personal, but be crafted based on the current desires and needs of the subscribers on your list. Instead of capping your coaching program based on the number of clients, you might cap it solely based on a beginning date, so the scarcity you build in will look a little different.

In the preceding pages, I've given you a handful of sample emails written as templates; in the next few pages, I've literally copied current emails from my own campaigns to give you even more ideas for how you can write emails. Hopefully, these sample emails spark your imagination and give you some ideas of what you can include and write about in your own emails; but always remember, each email you write can be unique, and there are no hard and fast rules for writing emails. The goal should be to connect with your subscribers and gain an intended action, such as building credibility, obtaining a sale, or generating a new client, and each email should be written to accomplish the chosen purpose.

MORE SAMPLE EMAILS

Here are a few emails from a current campaign of mine:

Intro Email (the first email someone receives when he joins my list):

Subject line:

Welcome to Sean Mize's Daily Coaching Tips . . .

Body of email:

(Prospect Name),

Welcome!

If you have a coaching program that you administer online, and you want to take it to the next level, you are in the right place!

Hi, my name is Sean Mize . . .

and since you are reading this, it means you have recently joined my coaching training email letter.

Basically what I do is once per day, for about 30 days, send you an informative email that (hopefully) teaches you something useful you can use in your coaching business.

Everything I will teach you in the first 30 days are things that I personally use in my own coaching business . . .

You will find that many of my techniques are so simple, yet when you implement them, you will get great results in your coaching program.

I will be teaching you easy methods of delivering your coaching . . .

. . . a super-simple way to outline a 13-week coaching program in less than one hour . . .

. . . how to use my secret email exchange method to find prospects fast . . .

. . . the exact outline of the script I personally used to close $5,000–$12,000 coaching clients . . .

. . . secrets of writing an email sequence to sell your coaching automatically . . .

. . . how to do an easy 30 day launch for your coaching business . . .

. . . and much, much more!

You will find that each day you are wishing that tomorrow's email would come . . . sooner!

Here is my advice to you:

Each day when I send you a training, read it, then ask: "how can I implement this in my business today to fast-track my coaching business?"

And of course—you may find that you want deeper instruction on each of my techniques than you can receive in a 200-word email—and you might want to consider enrolling in one of my high-level coaching training courses . . . but of course that is optional . . . if you apply what I send you in the email training, you can double or triple your coaching income fast!

Ok, that's all for today . . .

Tomorrow . . . the roots of my coaching system . . . how to build your coaching business 3–5x faster using my proven simple system . . .

Till tomorrow,

Sean Mize
http://www.30daycoachingbusiness.com

Credibility Email (this is an email that shows I am credible as an information source):

Subject line:

An article about keyword targeting . . . .

Body:

(Prospect Name),

Some time ago, ezinearticles published
an article I wrote about keyword targeting . . .
and I think it's as relevant today as it was then,
so check it out:

http://ezinearticles.com/?SEO-Keywords-in-Article-Marketing-and-SEO---Why-Keyword-Targeting-Doesnt-Work&id=5239746

To your success,

Sean Mize

Content-Based Email:

Subject line:

Do you have a burning desire to help people, to really change the world?

Body:

(Prospect Name), I had a thought this morning—

I'll share it in just a second, but first
a little background—

Sometimes I get to wondering, why do
some people never get going online,
and why do others succeed?

And of course there are usually some
pat answers that come to mind . . .
you know, some people work harder,
some people are smarter, etc.

But let's face it . . . you work hard at building
your business and you are smarter than
a lot of the people you see making a living
online, right?

And it's really frustrating that no matter how hard you work, no matter how much you learn . . . you are still struggling to take your business to $10k a month, right?

And that's what I've been thinking about . . . why . . .

And then I thought—what about my own clients?

And then it hit me:

My clients who are doing really well—the ones making a full-time income online—they are not just selling something . . . they are helping people do something they LOVE to help with—

Let me clarify—I don't know of a single client, who has the singular goal of getting rich, that is growing quickly in his coaching business . . .

BUT . . . my clients who really love helping people in their niches . . . like my fitness-instructor client who is improving clients' lives, my animal-health client who is growing leaps and bounds, my copywriting client who is teaching others how to do what he does well . . .

my business coach who is changing clients' lives . . . I could go on and on . . .

they are ALL doing it because they LOVE it— and then the money follows.

So . . . what about you?

Do you have a burning desire of something you want to help people with?

Do you have a burning desire to help people?

Do you have a burning desire to change the world?

Or are you just trying to find a way to "get rich online"?

Look, I know this is counterintuitive—but if you have as your goal "to get rich"—you probably won't get there.

But . . . if you start going out of your way to help people —really help them— you can create a HUGE internet business helping people in your niche.

Okay, once again—the goal is to HELP PEOPLE—
the more people you help, the more money
you will make.

So . . . how are you going to help people?

Do you really want to help people?

How many people are you going to help
in the next year?

How many lives are you going to change????

(Prospect Name), I sure hope
this has been helpful to you . . . .

I hope you clarify your dream and how you
can help people—so that you can
take the next year to a new level!

In fact, I challenge you—the next few days—
take some time for yourself—and focus on
finding that clarity—

How can you help others?

And how can you cultivate that desire?

Once you have that in place, the actual steps—the pillars of internet marketing—are really easy to implement.

(one of the hardest parts of this business is clarifying your desire and how you can really help people change their lives . . . once you get that, everything else is just a matter of plugging in the formula)

To your success,

Sean Mize

Sales Email:

Subject line:

Do you want to master your autoresponder?

Body:

(Prospect Name),

Here's the thing:

A critical component of your success is your ability

to automatically send emails to your subscribers.

If you don't, you will lose track of people and forget to send them the correct message at the right time.

When someone comes onto your list, she should go through a minimum 90-day totally-planned-out campaign that specifies which day she gets which email.

The advantage to this is that you can use your autoresponder tracking to identify good and bad emails over time and improve your campaign.

Anyhow, I teach you how to do all of this in my autoresponder mastery training:

http://www.emailfunnelmastery.com

You'll also learn:

--> How to Write Your First 10 Credibility Emails in Your Campaign (get these wrong and you will lose subscriber credibility fast).

--> How to Write a Product Launch Campaign (prelaunch, during launch, and post-launch).

--> *Step-by-Step How to Write*
Your 100-Day Email Campaign
for Maximum Sales.

Check it out here:

http://www.emailfunnelmastery.com

Sean

Obviously, those are just examples, but hopefully they give you an idea of how creative you can be in writing your own email sequence. One of the things that was really helpful to me when I first started writing emails was thinking about what an individual subscriber might be looking for or might find useful, then writing the email as if writing just to that subscriber, and then sending that email to my entire list. This tends to make the email seem more personal than if you are mentally writing to "the list" instead of writing to a person. In any case, I encourage you to start writing emails, and allow them to improve over time!

GET PROSPECTS ON YOUR EMAIL LIST

Now that you have an email campaign created, it's time to get prospects to become subscribers so they can move through your campaign, build trust in you, and eventually enroll in coaching or purchase your home-study courses.

In order to get people to subscribe to your email list, you need to have a mechanism to get them to subscribe. You can either place an opt-in form (that's a form that is provided by your autoresponder service that prospects use to add themselves to your email list) on your website or blog with an incentive to subscribe, or you can create a dedicated page with an incentive to subscribe, otherwise known as a squeeze page.

I prefer to use a squeeze page rather than just an opt-in form because conversion rates tend to be higher with a squeeze page. Because a squeeze page has as its only purpose the opting-in of subscribers, don't include additional ways for someone to take action on this page, other than to opt-in to your email list. If you have other actions for people to take on this page, for example, going to your blog or getting more information about you, they will generally take that (easier) option instead of opting-in to your email list.

CREATE A SQUEEZE PAGE

There are several ways to create a squeeze page. If you know how to design a web page already, you can create it in your favorite software. Or you can create it through your autoresponder service. Or if you want to create a squeeze page on a website but don't know how, get web hosting, search for "squeeze page templates" online, find one you like that comes with complete directions for customizing and uploading, buy it, and customize and upload the squeeze page (it will require a bit of a learning curve, but it will be well worth it once you learn how).

Here are the basic elements of a squeeze page:

- A relevant headline. This will be the first thing someone sees on your squeeze page, and should have a compelling offer that persuades your visitor to read the rest of the page. It is typically written in a larger type size than the rest of the type on the page, so that it stands out. Here is an example:

Discover the Secret to (Doing Something in Your Niche)

- A sub-headline. The sub-headline will give additional supporting information about what the offer will do for the reader, for example:

7 Step Plan for (Doing Something in Your Niche)

or

Download a Free Ebook Today to Learn How to (Do Something in Your Niche)

- 4–7 bullet points explaining what someone will receive when he opts-in to your list. These bullet points should each describe one detail of what he will learn or receive when he opts-in. For example:

    - Learn how to . . .
    - Discover my secret to . . .
    - Get my 4 resources for . . .
    - Do this today and get more (something in your niche)
    - Learn how to . . .

- A call to action (instructions to opt-in) and your web form from your autoresponder account. For example:

    Simply enter your name and email below and I'll immediately give you access to my weekly "Secret of the Week Newsletter" and send you my free guide "Discover the Secret of (Something in Your Niche)":

    (web form for someone to opt-in to your list)

On the following page is a sample squeeze page template to show how it all fits together:

SAMPLE SQUEEZE PAGE TEMPLATE:

Discover the Secret to (Doing Something in Your Niche)

Download my 7 Step Plan for (Doing Something in Your Niche):

- Learn how to . . .
- Discover my secret to . . .
- Get my 4 resources for . . .
- Do this today and get more (something in your niche)
- Learn how to . . .

Simply enter your name and email below and I'll immediately give you access to my weekly "Secret of the Week Newsletter" and send you my free guide "Discover the Secret of (Something in Your Niche)":

(web form for someone to opt-in to your list)

That's it. It is totally customizable for your niche and offer. Feel free to design your own or use the above example (customizing for your niche).

THE INCENTIVE TO SUBSCRIBE

To get your prospects to subscribe, create a digital incentive to give away to new subscribers. You can write a 7- to 25-page intro guide or record a 10- to 15-minute audio that teaches whatever you have promised on the squeeze page, and gives some information about yourself, your expertise, and how you can help.

To write the intro guide, create an outline of the answers to 5–7 key problems or challenges in your niche. Write approximately 1–5 pages per problem or challenge discussing how to solve those problems or challenges. Convert the intro guide into a pdf, then upload it to your website or attach it to the first email in your email campaign.

To record a 10- to 15-minute audio, use the above-mentioned outline, but instead of writing 1–5 pages per topic, record 2–5 minutes per topic. Upload the audio to your website, or attach it to the first email in your email campaign. (For more detailed technical instructions for creating and uploading your squeeze page, and for creating and uploading the digital incentive, go to AnyoneCanCoach.net.)

Key Points

- To get prospects to join your email campaign, offer a digital incentive, such as a short ebook, a short audio, or a short video.
- Create a squeeze page where prospects can request your digital incentive and be added to your email campaign.
- Building trust online is similar to building it offline —it requires credibility, consistency, and time.
- You can write an extended email campaign and deliver it using an autoresponder service to create credibility and trust, and to promote your products and coaching programs.

Recommended Reading:

The 7 Triggers to Yes by Russell H. Granger

Recommended Training:

primalbonding.com
recommendedautoresponders.com
emailfunnelmastery.com
autorespondermastery.com

Get more at AnyoneCanCoach.net

Chapter 13

Attract Prospects

Marketing using both online content and paid advertising will create a steady supply of new prospects coming into your email campaign.

I'm going to share with you some of the easiest and most popular ways to find prospects, but first I want to express the idea that finding prospects doesn't have to be more complex than simply "going where they are," whether that is where they are searching for help, or where they are congregating. I find it is helpful to think in terms of the question "how can I find where my prospects congregate?" rather than "how can I 'get traffic'?" Your prospects are real people looking for a real solution; they are not just some "click" or "visitor." So as I share these methods with you, and as you begin to implement them, keep in mind that although I am systematizing the steps for finding prospects, it is only to simplify the process. But at its core, marketing is simply the process of positioning yourself to find prospects "where they are," so you don't necessarily have to do "marketing" a certain way just because it's the way I do it or the way someone else does it. Instead, think in terms of finding prospects where they are, and think of these techniques I will show you as being a systematized cross section of the huge and ever-changing number of ways you can find and attract prospects.

With that in mind, I'll start by showing you how to find prospects using content marketing, which is the process of using content such as articles, audios, and videos to find prospects; then I'll show you a few ways to find prospects using advertising, which is the process of using paid methods such as email and cost-per-action marketing to find them.

CONTENT MARKETING OVERVIEW

When you create content such as articles, blog posts, audios, or videos, and post it online, people are attracted to it either directly, such as by the search engines, or indirectly, such as by other sites referencing it online. If a prospect likes what he reads or hears in the content and he wants to learn more from you, he can click through a link in your content that leads to your squeeze page where he can join your subscriber list and be added to your email campaign.

Here is an example of how it works: A search engine leads your prospect to an article you have written and posted to an online blog or website. Your prospect reads the article, likes what he has read, and wants to read more. He clicks the link at the end of the article that leads to your squeeze page, he opts in to your email campaign, and he receives your free giveaway guide. He might also click a link to another website where you have posted additional articles, and after reading a few more articles written by you, he begins to feel a level of respect for your credibility (which is established by your online presence). He may then search for your name online (in a search engine) and when he does, he finds you are featured on as many as 10–20 additional websites, which builds his respect for your credibility and perceived expertise.

At this point, he will likely be receptive to any marketing message you extend, especially if it is presented in such a way that it is a solution to his problem. If in the course of receiving your emails he continues to be given quality content that educates him instead of just being the same kind of sales pitch he might be receiving from your competition, he may begin seeking a solution from you. This sets up a long-term dynamic of your prospect seeking a solution from you, instead of you having to constantly market to him.

The process in this example involves the prospect reading a blog post, going to your squeeze page, becoming a subscriber, and receiving and reading your emails; it could be represented using this notation:

> blog post --> squeeze page --> subscribe -->
> receive and read emails --> become a client

However, this is only one of a limitless number of attraction paths someone could take.

Here are some examples of others:

- article --> blog post --> squeeze page --> subscribe --> receive and read emails --> become a client
- social media post --> article --> blog post --> article --> squeeze page --> subscribe --> receive and read emails --> become a client
- article --> social media post --> blog post --> squeeze page --> subscribe --> receive and read emails --> become a client

You can use any combination of the following elements to create a path for prospects to use to get to your squeeze page:

- articles
- web pages
- blog posts
- audios online
- videos online
- social media
- books, booklets, or ebooks

The more of these elements that you are able to link together online, the more credibility, perceived expertise, and ultimately, market exposure, you create. These do not need to be constructed overnight. Consider adding an instance of each element per day. For example, if you choose to use articles, blog posts, and social media posts, then each day you could write an article, a blog post, and a social media post.

Clients who spend at least a few minutes per day implementing these elements tend to be much more successful in the long run at creating online exposure than clients who try to work on these elements once per week or once per month. Over time, as your content base grows, you will begin to see how the various pieces of content are driving prospect engagement, and that will increase your desire to grow your content base. It's easier to see this growth when you are actively involved in creating content on a daily basis, as compared with once per week or once per month in marathon sessions.

HOW TO CONTENT MARKET

Many niche-specific websites and blogs are in need of content and blog-post writers. To find niche-specific websites and blogs online, use a search engine and search for terms like "(your niche) + websites" or "(your niche) + blogs." You can also search for relevant search terms in your niche. Go through the listings in the search engine. Take a look at each website. For each one that contains content similar to what you could contribute, for example, articles, blog posts, etc., ask yourself if your content or topic would be a good fit for that website or blog. If so, find the contact info on the site, and send an email to the editor or owner and ask if he would be interested in having you as a guest writer. Be prepared that many of your emails will go unanswered, and many sites will not need new writers. But if you are persistent, you will find websites that would welcome your help.

You might find a few websites that need a regular post written. You might agree to write one post per day, per week, or per month for these sites. The content topics and length of the posts will vary from website to website, and the amount of "self promotion" you can do in each website will vary. However, at the minimum, you should be able to put an author mini-bio or resource box at the end of each post or article, to lead readers to your squeeze page, to other instances of your content online, or preferably to both.

You can write articles and submit them to the various article directories (websites that accept article submissions as their primary content source). To find article directories, simply search online for "article directories," then follow the submission guidelines for each site.

You can write articles and put them on your own website or blog. If you do this, each time you write and submit an article or a blog post to other blogs and websites, include a link to an individual article on your own website in the mini-bio or resource box, in addition to a link to your squeeze page, to gain web exposure and develop search rankings.

This process of finding websites to write for is tedious; however, it will pay off in prospects and clients in the long run. And once you have found 5–10 sites to write for, you will simply be writing content for these sites, rather than writing emails to find sites.

HOW TO WRITE ARTICLES

DETERMINE THE TOPIC

If you are writing for a specific website, you may be assigned a topic. If you are not assigned a topic, you can write articles based on your 10 x 10 matrix. If you have a list of email subscribers in your niche, you can ask your subscribers what their biggest challenges are. Write articles that provide answers and solutions to those challenges.

You can also search for "(your niche) + forums" online. In most niches you will find forums where people are asking questions online. The questions people are asking are the questions your articles should answer.

You can also search for "(your niche) + questions," "(your niche) + answers," or "(your niche) + blogs" online. What people are already writing about in your niche is often what people are looking for. Once you know what people are looking for in your niche, you are assigned a topic, or you have topics from your 10 x 10 matrix, you can begin writing articles.

WRITE THE TITLE

Your title should specifically indicate the topic of the article. For example, "How to . . . (what you will teach in the article)." This is important because the title is the biggest determining factor when someone is deciding whether or not to read your article. And the more people who read your article, the more prospects you will generate in the long run.

WRITE THE ARTICLE

Write a paragraph that introduces your topic and tells the reader what he will learn by reading the article. You can write a sentence or two that reaffirms the topic of the article and tells what you will teach in the article, write a sentence or two that explains why the topic is important, and write a sentence or two listing out each of the main points in the article.

In the body of the article, teach what you have promised in the title and the introductory paragraph. You can write this in a few paragraphs; or you can create bulleted points, and in each bulleted point teach one idea or topic.

If you follow this formula, it's easy to quickly write 500- to 1,000-word articles. Think of writing the introduction in 100–200 words, then write 100–200 words for each topic or main idea you are teaching.

WRITE AN EFFECTIVE RESOURCE BOX

A resource box is a short blurb at the end of your article that publishers allow you to use to direct readers (visitors) to your squeeze page and other web content.

Here is a recommended resource box:

By the way, do you want to learn more about (topic of your article)? If so, download my brand new free ebook here: (url to squeeze page).

(Your Name) is an expert at (your niche).

The "By the way" transition helps connect the resource box with the article, which increases conversion. Tell the reader what he will receive if he chooses to go to your website. Don't write excessively about yourself. At this point, the reader probably isn't very interested in your accomplishments; instead, he is likely interested in solving his problem. He is reading your article because he wants to solve a problem, and he will generally only go to your squeeze page and opt-in because he wants more information about solving his problem, not because he wants more information about your accomplishments.

SAMPLE ARTICLE TEMPLATE:

Title

First paragraph: Introduction to your topic telling the reader what he will learn by reading the article. A sentence or two that reaffirms the topic of the article and tells the reader what you will teach in the article. A sentence or two that explains why it is important for the reader to understand what you will teach in the article, and a sentence or two listing out each of the main points in the article.

Second paragraph: Point 1; explain what it is, why it is important, and how to do it.

Third paragraph: Point 2; explain what it is, why it is important, and how to do it.

Fourth paragraph: Point 3; explain what it is, why it is important, and how to do it.

Fifth paragraph: Point 4; explain what it is, why it is important, and how to do it.

Sample Article Template (Continued)

Sixth paragraph: Point 5; explain what it is, why it is important, and how to do it.

Seventh paragraph: Point 6; explain what it is, why it is important, and how to do it.

Resource box: By the way, do you want to learn more about (topic of your article)? If so, download my brand new free ebook here: (url to squeeze page).

(Your Name) is an expert at (your niche).

VIDEO MARKETING

Video marketing is the process of recording short videos and posting them online to attract prospects to your website or squeeze page. To create a video, write a short outline of what you will teach, then teach from the outline. For a 10-minute video, this will likely be very similar to the article-writing formula: an introduction to the video topic, 3–7 supporting points, and a call to action at the end recommending the listener go to your squeeze page, download the digital incentive, and join your list. Using your computer and video-recording software, or using a portable video recorder, record the video, then upload it to one of the online video directories, or to your own website or blog.

SOCIAL MEDIA MARKETING

Social media marketing is the process of using social media sites to create awareness. This is normally done not so much through the process of driving traffic to specific web pages, but instead by building relationships through the social media sites, and then suggesting that people take action on your squeeze page. One of the easiest ways to do this is to write content (short articles or tips) and post it to your social media pages regularly, with directions at the end of each article or tip for going to your website (similar to using a resource box in commercially published articles).

FORUM MARKETING

Forum marketing is the process of building a reputation as an expert in your topic at the various niche-specific forums online. Start by finding the forums in your niche. Using a search engine, search for "forums + (your niche)"; for most niches, you should be able to find several forums.

Join each of the forums as a member, and begin to answer questions in the forum. Don't try to sell. Through the process of seeing you answering questions, people will begin to see you as an expert, and seek you out when they need help. In some of the forums you will be able to include a signature with your name and website or squeeze page url, and this will be enough to give interested people a contact point.

You don't need to ask them to go to your site, or offer them anything for going there (in fact, if you do, you will likely be banned from the forums, because the forums generally don't want advertising or self-promotion on their sites). The key is positioning yourself as an expert to people who need your expertise, and once that is in place, people will come to you.

BOOK MARKETING

When people read a book, booklet, or ebook you have written, they'll often want to learn more from you by going to your website or squeeze page. To get traffic from your book, give directions in the book to go to your website. You can also offer additional reading material, bonus resources or tools, or other bonuses to incentivize readers to go to your website.

USING PAID ADVERTISING

So far, all of the traffic sources I have shared with you have been content-based, organic sources which rely primarily on content writing and distribution, and although you might pay others to create or publish the content, the actual traffic generation is no or low cost. Next I will show you a few ways to use paid advertising sources to "speed up" your prospect generation. However, I recommend that you start with content marketing first, before you begin to do paid advertising, because the content marketing forms a credibility base for you, in addition to creating prospects. Once that credibility base is in place, you can consider speeding up traffic by utilizing these paid methods.

SOLO EMAIL ADS OR MAILINGS

A solo email ad is an advertisement that is sent to someone else's subscriber list on your behalf. One huge advantage to advertising on someone's email list as compared with advertising on a website is that if someone comes to your list as a result of reading someone else's email, you already know that this person opens, reads, and responds to email. This makes her an ideal prospect because you will be primarily marketing through email. Have the email list owner send his email readers to your squeeze page so that you can build a list of prospects, rather than trying to make a sale directly from the solo email ad. The email you will ask the list owner to send to his list might look like this:

Subject line:

Do you want to discover (something on your squeeze page)?

Body:

(Name of Recipient),

Do you want to discover (something relevant to your niche)?

If so, I'd like to introduce you to (your niche) expert (Your Name).

You can download his (or her) free guide to (something on your squeeze page here):

(url to squeeze page)

(Name of List Owner)

That is a simple email which you can easily customize to fit your niche and market. The list owners from whom you buy solo ad mailings will mail that email to their lists. As people read the emails and come to your squeeze page, they will opt-in to your list and become your subscribers and prospects.

To find people in your niche who are willing to do solo ads, search online for "(your niche) + solo ad" or "(your niche) + email solo ad." Another way to find people who are willing to do solo ads is to join subscriber lists in your niche, then ask each list owner if he would do a solo ad mailing for you. To find people in your niche who have a list, do an online search for your niche terms. Go through each link on the first 5–10 pages of the search results, joining any list you can. You can also search the paid links, and join lists there as well. Wait until you have been on the lists for 30–90 days, then send each list owner the following email:

Subject line:

Do you offer a paid mailing to your list?

Body:

Dear (List Owner's Name),

Hi, my name is (Your Name) and I have been on your list for some time now, and it seems that your list has a similar demographic to mine.

Would you be interested in doing a paid mailing to your list for me?

If so, please tell me how many subscribers you have, how many visits you normally generate from a mailing, and the cost to mail to your list.

Thanks,

(Your Name)

Those people who are willing to do solo ad mailings to their lists for you will respond and give you the details. Be prepared in advance that a small percentage will not be honest about their list size or responsiveness, so you won't get the same results on those mailings as you do with your other mailings. However, don't allow that to scare you, just recognize that over the course of doing multiple mailings, you will get good results. Simply make a note not to buy future solo ad mailings to the poor-performing lists.

EMAIL AD SWAPS

An email ad swap is very similar to a solo ad, but instead of paying someone to mail to her list, you mail to your list for her in exchange for her mailing to her list for you.

Email ad swaps can be an effective way of building your list; however, each mailing you do has an impact on your own list. If you do too many email ad swaps, your own subscribers feel cheated, and will unsubscribe from your list. Be sure that anytime you do an email ad swap your partner is giving real value to your subscribers.

It is easy to see quick results from ad swaps as your list builds, and to become too enthusiastic about doing them. You can easily burn your list out and ruin your reputation with your subscribers. However, when ad swaps are used carefully they can be powerful and give you great results.

To find email ad swap partners, join subscriber lists in your niche, wait 30–90 days, then ask each list owner if he would do an email ad swap with you. You can send each list owner an email like this:

Subject line:

Would you be interested in doing an email ad swap?

Body:

Dear (List Owner's Name),

Hi, my name is (Your Name) and I have been on your list for some time now.

It seems that your list has a similar demographic to mine.

Would you be interested in doing an email ad swap with me, where I will mail an offer to my list, recommending to my subscribers that they join your list, and you will mail an offer to your list, recommending that your subscribers join my list?

We both gain subscribers, and we are both able to add value to our subscribers and to our lists.

If so, shoot me an email, and let's organize an email ad swap.

(Your Name)

When you do the email ad swap, both you and your ad swap partner will simultaneously send to your respective lists an email similar to the solo email:

Subject line:

Do you want to discover (something on your squeeze page)?

Body:

(Name of Recipient),

Do you want to discover (something relevant to your niche)?

If so, I'd like to introduce you to expert (Your Name).

You can download his (or her) free guide to (something on your squeeze page here):

(url to squeeze page)

(Name of List Owner)

JOINT VENTURE OR AFFILIATE RELATIONSHIPS

A joint venture or affiliate relationship, in this context, is a relationship where you pay someone a percentage or flat fee for sending prospects or clients to you. In the case of a joint venture or affiliate partner sending you prospects, it is normally customary for you to pay a flat fee per prospect, or if he is mailing to his own prospect list, you might pay a flat fee for the mailing itself. If the joint venture or affiliate partner is sending you traffic that you will initially convert into product sales, then you could pay the joint venture or affiliate partner a percentage of sales. Of course, you could also pay a joint venture partner or an affiliate partner a percentage of the coaching sale itself, if you are marketing directly to her traffic source or email prospect list.

You can find affiliate or joint venture partners by mailing an email like this to list owners in your niche:

Subject line:

Would you be interested in a joint venture relationship?

Body:

Dear (Prospective Joint Venture Partner)

Hi, my name is (Your Name) and I have been on your list for some time now.

It seems that your list has a similar demographic to mine.

Would you be interested in developing a joint venture relationship, where we can enhance the value we give our lists, and possibly increase our profitability, by working together on some projects of interest to both of our respective lists and prospect bases, for example, email ad swaps, recommendations of each others' products or trainings, or possibly the creation of a product together?

If so, shoot me an email, and let's talk about how we can best work together.

(Your Name)

You can also find affiliate and joint venture partners at live events that relate to your niche, and then build relationships that culminate in you and your partners working together to build your businesses (through cross promotion, you to their lists, them to your list).

When the joint venture or affiliate partner mails for you, have him use an email similar to the solo email:

Subject line:

Do you want to discover (something on your squeeze page)?

Body:

(Name of Recipient),

Do you want to discover (something relevant to your niche)?

If so, I'd like to introduce you to expert (Your Name).

You can download his (or her) free guide to (something on your squeeze page here):

(url to squeeze page)

(Name of List Owner)

COST-PER-ACTION (CPA) MARKETING

Cost-per-action (CPA) marketing is the process of paying for traffic only when it produces a result, such as a subscriber or a prospect. CPA marketing is often simply a paid version of a content marketing channel. For example, the purpose in content marketing is to get people to see your articles, blog posts, etc. when they are searching for information. With CPA marketing, you can purchase those views, for example, by buying search engine listings, links on websites, or links to articles, blog posts, or videos. Instead of the visitor finding your content organically by searching online, you are paying for search engines or websites to directly send the visitor to your site or content.

FINDING PROSPECTS OFFLINE

You can also find prospects offline, right in your town or neighborhood. To find them, create flyers or brochures that lead to your squeeze page; offer local workshops or seminars; or use speaking engagements where you do a 90 minute informative talk about a topic that is useful to your ideal prospect, then send attendees to your squeeze page at the end of the talk, or offer a one-on-one free consult with people who are interested in learning more about working with you.

OUTSOURCING TRAFFIC GENERATION

To outsource traffic, hire people to do the individual tasks you find yourself doing in the traffic process. For example, you write articles, so hire someone to write articles. You submit those articles online, or upload them to your site, so hire someone to submit and/or upload the articles. You purchase traffic from various sources, so unless you are using traffic channels that can be automated over time, you hire someone to buy and monitor the results of your advertising.

You might be asking, "Why not hire one person to do all the tasks?" There are several reasons why it is better to hire a different person to do each task instead of hiring an "all in one" person. First, it is much harder to find one person who can do all the tasks, than it is to find several people who are each trained in one of the areas in which you need help.

Because of the nature of the huge outsourcing market, you can easily hire people on a per-project or part-time basis. This makes it is easy to hire multiple people who each perform a task that is uniquely suited to that person's skill set. For example, instead of hiring one person to do 8 different tasks, and having him work for 40 hours a week, you can hire 8 people who each work 5 hours a week on one task. Because you are hiring each person to do one task, instead of hiring people who are skilled in 8 tasks, you can usually pay the part-time or per-project outsourcers significantly less than the person who does and manages it all.

It's also easier to replace one worker who is not performing well on one task, than to replace someone on whom you are relying to perform all tasks. With multiple one-task workers, you aren't relying on any one person for your business to operate; instead, you spread the risk significantly over multiple workers. As you grow your business, you can increase the investment per task, perhaps beginning with 5-hour workers, increasing over time to 40-hour workers, multiple 40-hour workers, and so on.

Keep in mind, the reason your business is growing in the first place is that you have a system that works. So when you grow, you should be exactly duplicating your system. You shouldn't start changing your system based on the capabilities of your workers; instead, you should hire workers based on the needs of your system, and have those workers fit into your system.

SOME ADDITIONAL THOUGHTS ON TRAFFIC

Although I've shared with you some of the more popular and most effective methods of generating traffic, there are other traffic sources you may choose to test over time.

Never assume a particular traffic source will be the one thing that will transform your business. Test each traffic source before investing extravagantly in it. Also, a traffic source that works well for you today may not work as well in the future.

Conversely, a traffic source that doesn't work well today may work better in the future, as your marketing becomes stronger. The more efficient your marketing becomes, the more traffic sources you can use profitably.

Sometimes it's better to have a smaller number of prospects with whom you connect intimately than a huge number of prospects whom you can barely get to know. By developing quality relationships, you can generate much more revenue per subscriber than by mass marketing without building relationships. Your profitability can be much higher by thoroughly marketing to a smaller group of prospects than by barely meeting the needs of a much larger group of prospects.

CHOOSE A FEW TRAFFIC METHODS TO START WITH

Now that I've given you a number of different ways to generate traffic and prospects, perhaps you are wondering, "Which of these traffic sources should I use or start with?" All of the traffic sources I have given you can generate quality prospects and coaching clients, but I recommend that you choose a few that feel comfortable for you, and try them out. If you find that you like a specific traffic source, focus on becoming good at generating traffic in that way. You will develop an affinity for a few sources of traffic, and you will find that as you learn more about each, your results will improve over time.

You could start with content marketing as your first source of traffic online. You can easily build a strong flow of subscribers by simply spending a couple of hours a day on content marketing. This could include writing articles and submitting them to niche sites and the big article directories, writing blog posts as a guest blogger for popular sites, and getting involved in forums and blogs where people in your niche congregate. Social media can also be used judiciously in the context of content marketing; you can get involved by creating useful content, as long as you don't spend hours socializing on the social media sites.

In the long run, content marketing will likely generate the traffic that will create the highest rate of return on both your time and money. It is also a great testing ground for your email campaign and selling process. Once you are getting strong, consistent results in content marketing, you can consider rolling out other forms of advertising such as CPA marketing and email solo ads.

IMPORTANCE OF VOLUME AND CONSISTENCY

When driving traffic, volume and consistency over time is important. For example, just writing 4 blog posts each day would give you 1,000 blog posts in a year; writing a 15- to 20-page ebook or manual each week would give you 50 ebooks or manuals in a year; and recording 2 interviews per week would give you 100 interviews in a year.

How many of your competitors have blogs with over 1,000 posts? How many of your competitors have over 1,000 articles posted online? How many of your competitors have over 50 15- to 20-page ebooks or manuals online? How many of your competitors offer unique and genuine niche-relevant content at Facebook (rather than just social discussion and shallow content)? How many of your competitors have a web app that is updated daily? How many of your competitors have published multiple books? How many of your competitors have been interviewed by over 100 different people? Which of those milestones could you achieve in one year and differentiate yourself from your competition?

I realize that may seem insurmountable right now and a year or two might seem like a really long time. But a year or two will come and go as you are building your business, whether you achieve something like this, or not.

Let's face it, people (and your prospects) value the appearance that you've "done more" than your competition. Sure, you might be a "better expert" than your competition (or even not as qualified as your competition) but that is very difficult for a prospect to quantify. Frankly, it's your word against your competition's.

But when your prospect visits your competitor's site and finds 5 articles, and visits your site and finds 1,000 articles; or finds that you have 100 interviews by different experts posted all over the web, and your competitor has 3 . . . who do you think he'll believe is the more qualified expert?

You need to not only focus on increasing your expertise, but to also focus on those things that lead others to believe you are an expert. You see, you can be the best in the world, but if no one knows it, you won't have clients. And the more content you create and post online, the more traffic you will create, and the greater level of expertise you will project.

Key Points

- You can use articles, blog posts, audios, videos, and other web content to attract prospects to your email campaign and coaching offers.
- You can use paid sources of advertising in addition to content-based marketing to drive more prospects to your website.
- You can purchase or exchange solo mailings to other coaches' or email marketers' email lists to promote your website.
- You can write books and create other information products for the purpose of creating awareness of your website or coaching.
- Plan to be consistent with your traffic generation, and focus on quantity as well as quality.

Additional Reading:

Changing the Channel by Michael Masterson and MaryEllen Tribby

Content Marketing: Think Like a Publisher — How to Use Content to Market Online and in Social Media by Rebecca Lieb

Key Points (continued)

Content Rules: How to Create Killer Blogs, Podcasts, Videos, Ebooks, Webinars (and More) that Engage Customers and Ignite Your Business by Ann Handley, C.C. Chapman, and David Meerman Scott

Managing Content Marketing: The Real-World Guide for Creating Passionate Subscribers to Your Brand by Robert Rose and Joe Pulizzi

Additional Resources:

contentmarketingfortraffic.com
articlemarketingfortraffic.com
trafficbymarlon.com
outsourcingfortimefreedom.com

Get more at AnyoneCanCoach.net

Chapter 14

Next: Implement

Now that you know what to do to build your coaching business, the next step is implementation: creating and selling your coaching program, building relationships with prospects, and growing your business into the future.

You now have my complete Anyone Can Coach virtual coaching model. Here's a concise review of the steps and a suggested order in which to do them:

Start by outlining your coaching topic, then coterminously focus on attracting prospects and writing emails for your email campaign. That might look like writing a few articles or blog posts each day to attract prospects, and writing an email each day to nurture the relationships with those prospects (prospects are only going to receive a few emails each week, so if you are writing one each day, you easily stay ahead of your first prospects).

As prospects become interested in your coaching, offer them free consults, talk with them about what they need, sign clients up one at a time, and coach those clients one at a time. As you gain more clients, offer all existing one-on-one clients access to your group coaching program, and enroll future clients into your group coaching program.

You could visualize the process like this: attract prospects with marketing --> enroll prospects in an email campaign --> offer free consults --> enroll prospects in coaching --> deliver coaching to your prospects. The beauty of this model is that you can start as small as you want, and scale as large as you want. It is your choice.

IMPLEMENTATION

Now that you know what to do and how to do it to create and launch your efficient coaching business, your next step is . . . simply doing it: implementing what you have learned. No matter how much you know, if you don't implement it, you won't grow and achieve your goals.

Some common roadblocks to implementation are time management issues, daily distractions, and procrastination problems; if you allow these roadblocks to control your plan or your time, you won't be as successful as if you can overcome these challenges and simply implement your goals. What works for me is creating a plan that includes everything I want to accomplish, and then focusing on doing the tasks or steps necessary to implement the plan. I find that is more effective than using elaborate time management techniques, positive affirmations, or just trying to muscle through it with sheer willpower.

Here's how to do it:

Start by determining what you want to accomplish and the steps and actions necessary to accomplish those goals. Then spend the first few hours of each working day on those necessary steps and actions. Instead of focusing on time management, simply focus on what's important and get it done first. You'll be more productive, get more done, feel more rested, have more clarity, and have more emotional energy by focusing on your goals instead of focusing on managing your time.

Here are the steps to making this work:

- Determine what you want to achieve (your goals).
- Design a plan for achieving each goal.
- Create a time-based schedule for accomplishing each goal.
- Spend the first portion of your day executing your plan.

To make this easier to visualize, imagine you have a short-term goal of creating and launching a new coaching program.

Your plan and time-based schedule might look like this:

- Research: 10 hours
- Outlining and preparation: 10 hours
- Recording actual training: 20 hours
- Writing sales letter: 10 hours
- Writing email campaign: 10 hours
- Driving traffic to campaign: 20 hours

That is a total of 80 hours of work for this project. Simply start at the beginning of the list of things that need to be done, and systematically work through it. Assuming you have 4 hours per day to work on it, the completion time should be 20 days.

For example, in the first 2 1/2 days (10 hours), do the research. In the next 2 1/2 days (10 hours), write the outline and prepare to record the lessons. Spend the next 5 days (20 hours) recording the training. And so on, and at the end of 80 hours of work (20 days), you will have created and launched a new coaching program.

Imagine if you were to create one new project each month, and implement it like this. At the end of one year, you might have 2 coaching programs, 4 audio home-study courses, hundreds of articles and content pieces online, and a thriving coaching business.

How would it feel to be that productive? What would it mean for you if you could set goals, create a plan to achieve them, and then simply implement the steps necessary to get these kinds of results? The truth of the matter is, if you are willing to follow through and implement this technique, you can be that productive!

This is the same method I have used in my business to write 13 ebooks, record dozens of products, launch multiple coaching programs, mentor hundreds of clients, and finally, write this book, all in just over 5 years.

CONTROLLING DISTRACTIONS

When you are working on your long-term goals each day, do nothing else. Close your email browser. Turn your phone off. Close the door on your home office and let your family know that you are not available. If your family doesn't respect your work time at home, get an office away from home. In most cities there are small offices for rent at extremely reasonable prices, and just a few months of high productivity will easily justify the expense.

If you work exclusively on the things in your plan, you aren't controlled by distractions. As long as you keep your email browser closed, your phone off, and know what your plan is for the day before you begin, you simply work your plan. It gets even easier over time because once you get used to being so productive, you won't want to go back to the old way!

STAYING FOCUSED

I'm sometimes asked, "How do you stay so focused to be able to do all of this?" The key for me is that I know exactly what I want to achieve, I have an intense desire to achieve it, and I've created a specific plan for achieving it; so on a day to day basis I'm simply implementing the plan. I don't have to become re-motivated on a daily basis, because my motivation is internal—I know what I want, I know what to do to get what I want, so I just do it.

When you have an intense desire to fulfill a crystal-clear purpose and you know the exact steps to take to achieve the fulfillment of that purpose, you can simply focus on implementing your plan; you don't have to focus on "staying motivated." You are internally motivated by your intense desire for achieving your purpose.

You don't need a lot of additional mental willpower and extraordinary focus if your desire for fulfilling your purpose is intensely strong and internally motivated. And because you have created a plan that includes what needs to be done each day to fulfill your purpose over time, you can use your energy on doing the steps to achieve your goals, rather than on "staying motivated" or "staying focused."

I encourage you to take steps today to begin planning your future, planning your coaching program, implementing your plans, and living the transformed life of your dreams!

Key Points

- To make it easier to launch and deliver your coaching program, make a plan and focus on your highest priority actions on a daily and weekly basis.
- Dreaming and planning alone don't create achievements; your business will only grow as big as you implement what you learn.
- It is your choice to take action and get results.

Recommended Reading:

The Success System that Never Fails by W. Clement Stone

The Pledge: Your Master Plan for an Abundant Life by Michael Masterson

The Power of Full Engagement by Jim Loehr and Tony Schwartz

Think and Grow Rich by Napoleon Hill

Willpower by Roy F. Baumeister and John Tierney

Get more at AnyoneCanCoach.net

AFTERWORD

Now you know how to build your own coaching business. I've given you every step necessary to build a thriving coaching business; now it's your turn to create your coaching program and start selling it. You can do it!

I challenge you, if you haven't already begun to implement what I have taught you here, begin immediately. The single biggest challenge you will likely ever face in creating your coaching program is simply getting started.

Because you have read this far, I believe your desire is to create your own easy-to-run virtual coaching program. I believe you also desire the lifestyle that comes with running a 100%-virtual coaching business, and you desire to help others achieve their goals and dreams.

So take action. Begin your coaching program; design it the way you want. Enroll your first clients. Once you have taken these first steps, it becomes easier to scale and grow, helping more clients and growing your business quickly.

Coaching others to success using a systematized delivery system like I have taught you can be your key to the lifestyle of your dreams. Your next step is to just do it; empower others and live the life of your dreams!

To your success in your coaching business and your life!

Sean Mize

ABOUT THE AUTHOR

Sean Mize is an achievement strategist, long-time entrepreneur, and the creator of the *30 Day Coaching Business*, *InfoBusiness Automation*, and *Results and Freedom* training programs. He has launched multiple successful businesses, created multiple training courses and coaching programs, and mentored hundreds of clients.

Additional training programs by Sean:

How to Create a Coaching Business in 30 Days:
30daycoachingbusiness.com

Free Consult Selling System:
freeconsultsellingsystem.com

How to Create an Automated InfoBusiness:
infobusinessautomation.com

Primal Bonding Training Course:
primalbonding.com

Results and Freedom (Life Results) Training:
resultsandfreedom.com

Index

Made in the USA
Charleston, SC
13 March 2012